PREDESTINATION, GOD'S FOREKNOWLEDGE, AND FUTURE CONTINGENTS

99 98 97 96 95 94 93   3 4 5 6 7 8 9 10

Second edition 1983

Printed in the United States of America
Cover design by Laszlo J. Balogh

Hackett Publishing Company, Inc.
P.O. Box 44937
Indianapolis, Indiana 46244-0937

Library of Congress Cataloging in Publication Data
William, of Ockham, ca. 1285-ca. 1349.
    Predestination, God's foreknowledge, and future contingents.

    Translation of: Tractatus de praedestinatione et de praescientia Die et
de futuris contingentibus.
    Bibliography: p.
    Includes index.
    1. Predestination—Early works to 1800. 2. Logic—
Early works to 1800. I. Adams, Marilyn McCord.
II. Kretzmann, Norman. III. Title.
B765.O33T73 1982   234'.9   82-23317
ISBN 0-915144-14-X
ISBN 0-915144-13-1 (pbk.)

The paper used in this publication meets the minimum requirements of American
National Standard for Information Sciences—Permanence of Paper for Printed Library Materials, ANSI Z39.48-1984.

∞

PREFACE

In this volume we are presenting the first English translation of William Ockham's *Tractatus de praedestinatione et de praescientia Dei et de futuris contingentibus*. The three Appendices contain the first complete English translations of closely related discussions from Ockham's *Commentary on the Sentences of Peter Lombard, Commentary on Aristotle's* De interpretatione, and *Summa logicae*. Except for the translation of Chapter 9 of Aristotle's *De interpretatione* in Appendix II, all the translations are based on the editions prepared by Philotheus Boehner, O.F.M. These editions were published in *The Tractatus de Praedestinatione et de Praescientia Dei et de Futuris Contingentibus of William Ockham. Edited with a Study on the Medieval Problem of a Three-Valued Logic* ("Franciscan Institute Publications" No. 2); St. Bonaventure, N.Y.: The Franciscan Institute, 1945. We gratefully acknowledge the permission granted us by the Franciscan Institute to publish these translations.

We are especially grateful to Barbara Ensign Kretzmann and Robert Merrihew Adams, who helped in many ways in the preparation of this book.

Marilyn McCord Adams
Norman Kretzmann

Ann Arbor and Ithaca

TABLE OF CONTENTS

PREDESTINATION,
GOD'S FOREKNOWLEDGE,
AND FUTURE CONTINGENTS

INTRODUCTION

OCKHAM'S LIFE AND THE DATE OF THE *TREATISE*

William Ockham, a highly influential philosopher of the four-teenth century and one of the most important logicians of the Middle Ages, was born before 1290 (c.1285), probably in the village of Ockham, near London. He entered the Franciscan order while still quite young and began studying theology at Oxford around 1309, when the work of Duns Scotus (d.1308) was very influential here. We have no reason to think that the pattern of Ockham's years at Oxford deviated from the course normal for students of theology at that time: five years of study followed by two years of cursory lectures on the Bible, two more years of lectures on the *Sentences* of Peter Lombard, and a four-year period during which no teaching was done but preaching and formal disputation were allowed. Ockham commented on the *Sentences* between 1317–19, thereby attaining the rank of formed bachelor (*baccalarius formatus*). Although he spent the following two years completing the requirements for a master of theology degree, Ockham never became a regent master (*magister actu regens*), oc-cupying the Franciscan chair, because others were in line ahead of him and because his appointment was opposed by the chancellor of the university, John Lutterell. Probably, after finishing his studies, Ockham went to the *studium generale* of the London Cus-tody, where he taught and wrote philosophy until 1324, complet-ing all of his nonpolitical works. In 1323 Lutterell appeared be-fore the pope in Avignon with a list of 56 allegedly heretical theses taken from Ockham's writings. Ockham was summoned to

Avignon to answer these charges in 1324. After two years' deliberation, a papal commission found 51 propositions open to censure, although none was formally condemned by the pope. Toward the end of his four years in Avignon, however, Ockham became involved in a quarrel between the Franciscan order and the pope, John XXII, over Franciscan poverty. Assigned to research the issue by the minister general of the order, Michael of Cesena, Ockham concluded that John XXII had contradicted the Gospels and earlier papal pronouncements and was thus no true pope. Fearing an official condemnation of their position, Ockham and other leading Franciscans left Avignon in 1328, taking the seal of the order with them, whereupon they were excommunicated. In Pisa they came under the protection of Louis of Bavaria, whose election as Holy Roman Emperor the pope did not recognize. Settling with Louis at Munich, Ockham wrote many political treatises against John XXII and his successors. According to his epitaph, Ockham died at Munich on April 10, 1347, perhaps of the black plague.

Ockham's *Treatise on Predestination, God's Foreknowledge, and Future Contingents* was written before 1324, about the same time as the *Summa Logicae* (and hence as the material in our Appendix III), and a couple of years after the completion of his *Ordinatio* (Book I of his *Sentence*-commentary) and *Perihermenias*-commentary (and hence after the passages in our Appendices I and II, respectively).[1]

ANALYSIS OF THE *TREATISE*

Ockham's main business in this *Treatise* is to resolve problems for Christian theology, arising from its acceptance of the philosophical claim that some things are both future and contingent.[2] Briefly, an event, action, or state of affairs is contingent, if and only if it is both possible for it to be and possible for it not to be.[3]

---

[1]For further information on Ockham's life and works, see Gedeon Gál, "William Ockham," *The New Catholic Encyclopedia*, McGraw Hill, N.Y., 1967, vol.14. pp.932–5, as well as his introductions to the new critical editions of Ockham's works.

[2]For information on treatises of this sort before Ockham, see J. Groblicki, *De scientia Dei futurorum contingentium secundum S. Thomam eiusque primos sequaces.* Cracow: University Press, 1938; and J. Isaac, *Le Peri Hermeneias en Occident de Boèce á Saint Thomas,* Paris: J. Vrin, 1953.

[3]The senses of 'necessary', 'possible', 'contingent', and 'impossible' most relevant to the discussion in the Treatise are explained more precisely on pp. 5–7 below.

Ockham takes it to be part of Christian doctrine (i) that 'Peter will be saved' and the like are future contingent propositions, and (ii) that God has infallible foreknowledge of future contingents. But Aristotle's fatalistic arguments in *De interpretatione,* Chapter 9, seem to imply that (i) and (ii) are incompatible.[4] Ockham responds by developing a view regarding truth and future contingents which he uses to deal with other problems about predestination and God's foreknowledge as well.

The remainder of this Introduction provides some background for a study of Ockham's *Treatise.* We shall begin (in Part I) with his exposition of Aristotle's fatalistic arguments, together with his solution of the problems arising from them. Then (in Parts II–IV) we shall see how Ockham applies his view about truth and future contingents to handle four related topics.

I. Fatalism, God's Foreknowledge, and Predestination:

Briefly, fatalism is the view that whatever happens must happen of necessity and whatever does not happen of necessity does not happen at all. According to the fatalist, it is never both possible that something will happen and possible that it will not happen. That is, the fatalist denies that any events, actions, or states of affairs are contingent. It is generally taken to be an obvious consequence of fatalism that nothing a man does is ever really up to him. What he has done he had to do; and what he will do he must do.[5]

Many philosophers, including Aristotle, have thought that this highly implausible conclusion could be deduced from apparently impeccable principles of logic. In his *De interpretatione,* Chapter 9, Aristotle argues for this conclusion along the following line. Every singular proposition,[6] whether about the past or about the future, is either true or false. (The generalized form of this prin-

---

[4] A translation of the medieval Latin text of this chapter is included as part of Appendix II, pp. 96–109 below. Cf. J.L. Ackrill's translation of the original Greek in *Aristotle's Categories and De Interpretatione,* Oxford: Clarendon Press, 1963.

[5] On fatalism see Antony Flew's article "Precognition" (*Encyclopedia of Philosophy,* Vol. VI, pp. 436–441, especially, pp. 438–39) and Richard Taylor's article "Determinism" (*Encyclopedia of Philosophy,* Vol.II, pp. 359–373).

[6] A singular proposition is a proposition the subject term of which is a proper name or a definite description—e.g., 'Socrates', 'the man to whom you introduced me yesterday', 'her only brother'.

ciple is sometimes called "the principle of bivalence" because it recognizes only two truth-values, excluding for propositions any middle ground between being true and being false. It is sometimes described as a "law of thought" because it has been commonly taken to be not only unexceptionable but also one of the principles on which all reasoning is founded.) Consider some singular proposition about the future—'The Empire State Building will be colored white on January 1, 2068'. Either that proposition is true or it is false. But, so the reasoning goes, if it is true now that the Empire State Building will be colored white at that time, then nothing that can occur between now and January 1, 2068, can prevent it from being colored white then. In fact, if it is true now that the Empire State Building will be colored white on January 1, 2068, then it always was true. Consequently, it never was possible for anything or anyone to prevent the Empire State Building from being colored white at that time. On the other hand, if that proposition is now and always has been false, then it never was possible for anything or anyone to bring it about that the building will be colored white then. Thus, if it is now and always has been true that the Empire State Building will be colored white at that time, then the Empire Building will *of necessity* be colored white at that time; and if it is now and always has been false that the building will be colored white at that time, then it is *impossible* that the Empire State Building will be colored white on January 1, 2068. No matter how much anyone deliberates about the color of the building, no matter what steps are taken to give it that color then or to prevent it from having that color, it will make no difference. What will be will be of necessity. Obviously, if these observations hold regarding our example, they hold regarding any and every singular proposition about the future. But every event, action, or state of affairs either is now or was at some time future. The general conclusion, then, is that no events, actions, or states of affairs are contingent.

The crux of this line of reasoning is the inference from the hypothesis that a singular proposition of the form 'x will be A at tn' is true (or is false) at every time prior to tn to the conclusion that at tn x will be A (or will not be A) necessarily. Many philosophers have challenged this step in the argument. In his commentary on *De interpretatione*, Chapter 9, Ockham understands the inference as depending on special notions of modality, truth, and falsity.[7]

---

[7]Ockham's interpretation of Aristotle's two arguments is substantially the same as that of Boethius and Thomas Aquinas. G.E.M. Anscombe has contested this

The modalities at issue are not logical, but real: p is contingent in the relevant sense, if and only if there is a potency in things (*in rebus*) for p and a potency in things for not-p; necessary, if and only if there is no potency in things for not-p; and impossible, where there is no potency in things for p. From one side, such potencies are measured causally: if something is causally sufficient for p, there is no potency in things for not-p and p is necessary; but where nothing is causally sufficient for p and nothing for not-p, there is a potency for each (*potentia ad utrumlibet*) in things and p is contingent. From another side, contingency may be identified with ontological indeterminateness, by appeal to the principle that

(T1) where there is a potency for opposites, the potency for p (not-p) does not survive the reduction of the potency for not-p (p) to act.

If in the past there was a potency for opposites — say a potency for Peter's denying Christ and a potency for Peter's not denying Christ — the one has now been actualized to the exclusion of the other — Peter's denial has cancelled whatever potency there was in things for his not denying Christ on that occasion. Thus, Ockham will say that merely past events, actions, or states or affairs, such as Peter's denial, are necessary,[8] not in the sense that their opposites — e.g., Peter's never having denied Christ — are logically impossible, but in the sense that there is no longer any potency in things for their being otherwise. To mark the distinction, some logicians referred to this as "necessity *per accidens.*"[9] Where the double potency of contingency remains, neither p nor not-p has been determinately actualized yet.

Thus, Ockham follows standard medieval interpretation when he ascribes to Aristotle

(T2) x's being A at tm is determinate at tn, if and only if there is no potency in things at tn for x's not being (having been, being going to be) A at tm.

---

traditional interpretation in her article "Aristotle and the Sea Battle" (*Mind*, Vol. LXV (1956), pp. 1–15), and much discussion has followed. See Part V of the Bibliographies below.

[8]E.g., Question I, Objection 2, p.38 below; cf. p. 38 below, n.14. See also Assumption 3, pp. 46–47 below.

[9]See William of Sherwood, *Introduction to Logic,* translated by Norman Kretzmann, University of Minnesota, 1966, chapter 1, section 23, p. 41.

along with the view that propositions are true or false according as they correspond or fail to correspond with reality.[10] Because, by (T2), everything past or present is determinate, propositions solely about the past or present have determinate truth-value. So do propositions about future things necessitated by past or present things. But since singular future contingent propositions represent a double potentiality or "gap" in actuality that has yet to be filled in, there must be a corresponding "gap" in truth-values.[11] That is,

(T3) 'x is (was, will be) A at tm' is determinately true at tn, if and only if there is no potency in things at tn for x's not being (having been, being going to be) A at tm,

and

(T4) 'x is (was, will be) A at tm' is determinately false at tn, if and only if there is no potency in things at tn for x's being (having been, being going to be) A at tm.[12]

Just as, by (T2), things (events, actions, states of affairs) are determinate (or indeterminate) only at a given time, so singular propositions are determinately true or determinately false (if at all), not absolutely, but at a given time.[13] Propositions about future contingents will not, so long as they are future, satisfy either (T3) or (T4) and so will be neither determinately true nor determinately false. This does not mean, Ockham cautions, that the disjunction of a singular future contingent proposition and its denial lacks truth value. Quite the contrary, it is always true, because future contingents will be rendered determinate one way or the other at the future time in question.[14]

Returning to Aristotle's fatalistic arguments, Ockham represents the key inference of the first in these words: "what happens fortuitously is no more determined to one part than to the other—i.e., no more determined to being than to not being. Therefore, if it is determined that this will be, or that it will not be, it happens not fortuitously but of necessity."[15] In view of the allegedly Aristotelian truth-conditions in (T3) and (T4), however,

[10]See Appendix II, p. 101 and 105.
[11]See Appendix II, pp. 105 and 106 below. See also *Treatise*, Assumption 5, pp. 47–48 below, and *Summa Logicae* II,c.33; OPh I, p. 317.
[12]See Appendix II, p. 105 below,
[13]See, e.g., Appendix II, p. 104 below.
[14]See Appendix II, p. 105 below,
[15]Appendix II, p. 98 below.

if 'x will be A' is determinately true now (or determinately false now), it is determinate now that x will be A (or determinate now that x will not be A). Therefore, if 'x will be A' is determinately true now (or determinately false now), there is now no potency in things for x not to be going to be A (for x being going to be A) and x will of necessity come to be A (or not come to be A). And in general, if every singular proposition about the future is either determinately true or determinately false, then nothing occurs (or fails to occur) contingently but all things occur (or fail to occur) of necessity.

Ockham exposes the nerve of Aristotle's second argument in this passage: "This argument is based on the proposition that a singular proposition true about the past is necessary. Therefore if 'this is white' is true now, ' "this will be white" was true' is necessary. Consequently, it is necessary that it happen, and it cannot come about otherwise."[16] If ' "x will be white" was true' is necessary about the past, then something actual in the past necessitated x's being white now, so that there was no potency in the way things were then for x's not being white now. It follows that x did not come to be white contingently but necessarily. Thus, if every singular proposition about the future is determinately true or determinately false, everything that happens happens necessarily.

Aristotle draws the further consequence that the efficacy of deliberation would be destroyed. For, on the medieval reading, he held that

(T5) future free actions are among the future contingents.

Ockham goes so far as to say that " . . . nothing of which the Philosopher speaks here is fortuitously contingent except what is in the power of someone acting freely or depends on such an agent . . ."[17] But if every singular proposition were either determinately true or determinately false, "there would be no need to deliberate or to take trouble, since from the fact that it is determined [it follows that] it will occur as it was determined from the outset, whether or not we deliberate."[18] Aristotle's reasoning is remarkably fallacious: if everything came to pass of necessity, our deliberations would come to pass just as necessarily as our actions. Nevertheless, (T3)–(T5) do combine with the original hypothesis—that every singular proposition is either determi-

[16]Appendix II, p. 99 below.
[17]Appendix II, p. 106 below.
[18]Appendix II, p. 101 below.

nately true or determinately false—to yield Aristotle's conclusion. On the medieval interpretation, he takes it to be a *reductio* ad absurdum of the original hypothesis; and, refusing to give up his belief in human freedom, he admits exceptions to the principle of bivalence where singular future contingent propositions are concerned.

As philosophers and logicians, Ockham and other medievals were fascinated with the idea that such a substantive metaphysical position as fatalism might follow from impeccable principles of logic together with plausible assumptions about truth-conditions. But their interest in Aristotle's fatalistic arguments was intensified when they saw how additional theological problems could be derived from them. Two sets of arguments advanced by Ockham's opponents in the *Treatise* do just that.

(a) Arguments (1), (2), and (4) in Question II, Article I of the *Treatise* (pp. 54–55) make use of Aristotle's arguments to challenge

(T6) God has determinate knowledge of future contingents.

Arguments (1) and (4) are substantially alike except that (1) omits the first premiss found in (4); both contend that if there are any future contingents (if anything is indeterminate), then God has no determinate knowledge of them. Replying to argument (1), Ockham acknowledges its Aristotelian underpinnings by citing his Assumption 5, where he has explained in detail how Aristotle's position yields a denial of (T6).[19] The reasoning developed there mirrors the account found in his commentary on Aristotle's *De interpretatione*, Chapter 9, where he explicitly concludes that Aristotle "would say that God does not know one part of such a contradiction more than the other; neither is known by God."[20]

Argument (2) goes the other way around: if God has determinate knowledge of one or the other part of a contradiction involving future contingents, then one or the other part is determinately true—i.e., the doctrine of God's universal foreknowledge entails the principle of bivalence as applied to all singular propositions. But as shown above,[21] it follows from the principle of bivalence together with the Aristotelian truth conditions (T3) and (T4) that deliberation is in vain.

---

[19]*Treatise*, p.55.
[20]Appendix II, p. 105 below; cf. *Summa Logicae* III (3), ch.30 (Appendix III, p. 110 below.)
[21]On pp. 10–11 above.

(b) The objector's argument in Question 1, Objection 2 (p. 38) of the *Treatise* begins with an appeal to the principle of the necessity of the past, which is then applied to the proposition 'Peter is predestinate.' The objector and Ockham agree that at least part of what that proposition means is that Peter will be granted supreme blessedness on the day of judgment. Thus, even though 'Peter is predestinate' is a present-tense proposition, consideration of it involves one in the Aristotelian problems regarding singular propositions about the future. The argument is to the effect that if 'Peter is predestinate' is true now, there will never again be any potency in the way things are for Peter's not being granted supreme blessedness in the future. But in that case Peter will be granted supreme blessedness necessarily, and his receiving supreme blessedness or eternal punishment in no way depends on his deliberation hereafter or, indeed, on any subsequent event, created or divine—which is contrary to the faith. The objector assumes in accordance with the faith that we must say that the truth or falsity of some propositions—and in particular of propositions about one's eternal destiny—depends in part on human deliberation and choice. And he intends to show that since it is only with respect to indeterminate things that deliberation and choice can conceivably make a difference, it must be the case that some propositions—such as 'Peter is predestinate'—are about indeterminate things and hence neither determinately true nor determinately false.

The strategy of the objection parallels that of Aristotle's *reductio* arguments. It begins with a specific application of the principle of bivalence to singular propositions about the future and from that principle, together with the Aristotelian truth conditions (T3) and (T4), deduces the conclusion (absurd from a fourteenth-century Christian point of view) that a man's receiving supreme blessedness or eternal punishment has nothing to do with his deliberation or choice. The rejection of that absurd conclusion leads the objector to an Aristotelian denial of the principle of bivalence as applied to singular propositions in the specific case of singular future contingent propositions.

Thus, all three of these objectors' arguments (the first and third considered under (a) and the second considered under (b) above) may be seen to depend more or less explicitly on Ockham's account of Aristotle's stipulations regarding determinate truth and determinate falsity.

The substance of Ockham's replies to these objections is dictated by the need to preserve the doctrine of God's universal foreknowledge in the face of the contention that (T5) future free actions are future contingents. Conceding the validity of these arguments, Ockham seems to regard them as a *reductio ad absurdum* of the Aristotelian truth-conditions on which they rest. He apparently reasons that if the Aristotelian conditions in (T2)–(T4) for being determinate, determinately true, and determinately false, respectively, are accepted, conclusions incompatible with truth and the faith must be granted; hence (T2)–(T4) must be replaced with others that permit an unproblematic application of the principle of bivalence to every singular future contingent proposition.

Ockham's alternatives can be reconstructed from his many remarks (in the *Treatise* and elsewhere) on the way in which singular future contingent propositions are determinately true and determinately known by God. For (T2), he substitutes

(T7) x's being A at tm is determinate at tn, if and only if *at some time or other* there is (was, will be) no potency in things for x's not being (having been, being going to be) A at tm,

which allows a thing future relative to tn to be determinate at tn, even if nothing real or actual in the past or present relative to tn necessitates its future existence, provided that something that exists *at some time or other* settles its future existence. By contrast with (T2), (T7) makes being determinate only trivially time-relative, because the fact that something—e.g., Peter's denial of Christ—is actual at some time or other suffices—on (T7)—to make it determinate at any and every time.

Assenting to the fundamental thesis of Aristotelian truth-theory—viz., that propositions are determinately true or determinately false as they correspond or fail to correspond with what is determinately actual—Ockham likewise replaces (T3) and (T4) with

(T8) 'x is (was, will be) A at tm' is determinately true at tn, if and only if at some time or other there is (was, will be) no potency in things for x's not being (having been, being going to be) A at tm

and

(T9) 'x is (was, will be) A at tm' is determinately false at tn, if and only if at some time or other there is (was, will be) no potency in things for x's being (having been, being going to be) A at tm,

which close the truth-value gaps where future contingents are concerned and restore the principle of bivalence. On Ockham's view, every singular future contingent proposition is either determinately true or determinately false, and the doctrine of God's universal foreknowledge is preserved.

Ockham insists that his solution does not compromise the efficacy of human deliberation and choice either. According to (T3) and (T4), the determinate truth (falsity) of a proposition at a time is settled by something real or actual in the past or present relative to that time and so is something past relative to any later time. Hence, if '*p* is true' is true (false) now, '*p* was true' will be necessary (impossible) at any later time; as Ockham's Aristotelian opponents stipulate,

> (T10) Every proposition true (false) about the present relative to one time has corresponding to it a necessary (impossible) proposition about the past relative to a later time.[22]

By contrast, (T8) and (T9) allow that where future contingents are concerned the past or present truth of a proposition may be something yet to be settled by what will become actual in the future. In such cases, Ockham says that the proposition is true in such a way that it can be false and can never have been true, since nothing real or actual excludes the potency for the opposite.[23] Thus, he maintains that (T10) applies only where "propositions are about the present as regards both their wording and their subject matter (*secundum vocem et secundum rem*)" and not otherwise.[24] Apparently, a proposition of whatever tense is about the future as regards its subject matter (*secumdum rem*), if it is exponible by such in the way in which 'God foreknew from eternity "Peter will deny Christ"' is. And Ockham concludes that "just as this or that future contingent contingently will be, so God knows that it contingently will be, for if He knows it, He can *not* know that it will be."[25] And if neither the past truth nor God's past foreknowledge of future contingents falls under the necessity of the past, the Aristotelian argument that His determinate knowledge of them would destroy the efficacy of human deliberation and choice, fails.

Thus, just as the objectors' arguments in Question I, Objection 2, and in (1), (2), and (4) of Question II, Article I, are based on the Aristotelian truth-theory (in (T3) and (T4)), so Ockham's replies are grounded on his own alternative theory (in (T8) and

[22]See Assumption 3, pp. 46–7 below.

[23]*Treatise.* q.1,p. 42; q.2.a.4. Part One, p.67.

[24]Assumption 3, pp. 46–7 below. Cf. *Ordinatio* I,d.38,q.1 P; Appendix I, p.92 below.

[25]*Treatise,* q.2,a.4 L, p.67.

(T9)). Several of the more important features of Ockham's truth-theory are brought out in Assumptions 2, 3, and 4 of the *Treatise*.

II. The Ontological Status of Predestination and Reprobation:

Another of the essential applications Ockham makes of his view of future contingents in the *Treatise* is to the problem of the nature of predestination (and reprobation). He takes particular pains to reject two theories relating to this problem. The first of these (Theory 1) is the view that predestination is a "real relation" (the relata of which are the predestinate person and God). The second (Theory 2) is the view that active predestination consists in and passive predestination depends on acts of God's will in the past—acts that, because they are past, cannot be changed and that, because they are acts of God's will, cannot be obstructed.

According to Theory 1, considered at the very outset of Question I of the *Treatise,* to say that a person is predestinate now is to say, at least in part, that there is something real—the form of passive predestination—inhering in that person now. The inherence of this real form necessitates that person's receiving supreme blessedness on the day of judgment. Thus from 'Peter is predestinate' one may validly infer 'On the day of judgment God will give Peter supreme blessedness.' Moreover, according to Theory 1, the truth now (at *tn*) of 'Peter is predestinate' is settled by what is actual at *tn*—viz., the inherence of the form of passive predestination in Peter. Consequently, at any time *tm* after *tn* 'Peter was predestinate' will be necessary. Thus at any time *tm* after *tn* it will be necessary that on the day of judgment God will give Peter supreme blessedness.

On the basis of this consequence Ockham proceeds to reduce Theory 1 to an absurdity, employing the strategy to be found both in his reply to Question I, Objection 2, and in Assumption 2. His own position, the indirect conclusion of the *reductio ad absurdum,* is that there is no form of passive predestination inhering in Peter at or before *tn* in virtue of which 'Peter is predestinate' is true at *tn*.

Theory 2 is embodied in Question I, Objections 3 and 3a, where it is invoked as the basis of an attempt to reduce to an absurdity the view that the predestination or reprobation of any person is something to be settled by what will be actual in the future. To say that Peter is predestinate is, as the word 'predestinate' suggests, to say that God has in the past determined Peter's eternal destiny by an act of His will. Since God has willed that Peter is to be saved, if Peter can thereafter by an act of his own will commit the sin of final impenitence and thereby bring about his own damnation, it follows that God's will can be obstructed by Peter's will. But this is inconsistent with the doctrine of divine omnipotence, according to which 'God wills that p is true' entails 'p is true', and hence absurd. Thus, if what has been actual in the past settles it that God willed that p be true, in such a way that there is now no potency in things for His willing that p be false, it has also been settled that p is true, in such a way that there is now no potency in things for p's falsity. If God has willed that Peter will be saved, then, since God is omnipotent, Peter follows the divine will necessarily and *cannot* commit the sin of final impenitence that would bring about his damnation.

Ockham's rejection of Theory 2 is best understood in the light of a distinction between the antecedent and consequent disposing will of God. Although Ockham never introduces this distinction explicitly in the *Treatise,* a number of his remarks seem to presuppose it.[26] In *Ordinatio,* Distinction 46, Question I, B, Ockham takes note of this and other technical distinctions regarding the divine will: "it is commonly said that the will of God is twofold—viz., the disposing will (*voluntas beneplaciti*) and the revealed will (*voluntas signi*). [The revealed will] is distinguished into these five: prohibition, precept, counsel, fulfillment, and permission. Similarly, the disposing will is distinguished into the antecedent and consequent will."[27] The revealed will consists of God's commands to men and is not at issue here. The disposing will of God is whatever God is pleased to bring about. Regarding the *consequent* disposing will Ockham says that it is that "by which God wills efficaciously in positing something in being."[28] According to Christian doctrine nothing is brought about ("posited in being") or continues to be unless God wills that it be brought about or continue. That is, as regards the consequent disposing will of God, 'p is true' entails 'God wills that p is true'. On the other hand, Ockham observes that "nothing occurs contrary to the consequent disposing will of God," since "the will of God is omnipotent and not capable of being obstructed."[29] Thus, it is also the case regard-

---

[26]E.g., in his replies to Question I, Objection 3,3a, and 5, and in Assumptions 1 and 6.

[27]*Ordinatio* I,d.46,q.1 C.

[28]Ibid.

[29]*Ordinatio* I,d.46,q.1 D; similar remarks occur also at B and E.

ing the consequent will that 'God wills that p is true' entails 'p is true'. In effect, then, Ockham characterizes the consequent will in such a way that the proposition 'it is the consequent will of God that x is A at tn' is *equivalent* to the proposition 'x is A at tn.' Therefore, if Peter's receiving supreme blessedness on the day of judgment is not only future but also contingent—i.e., not settled by something actual in the past or present, so that there is now no potency for the opposite—then the consequent will of God regarding that state of affairs is likewise not settled by something actual in the past or present, so that there is now no potency for the opposite.

Nevertheless, according to Ockham there are determinations of the divine will regarding future contingents that *are* settled from eternity—viz., those designated jointly as "the antecedent disposing will of God." Of this aspect of God's will he says that it is "that will by which God gives to someone natural properties (*naturalia*) or antecedent conditions (*antecedentia*) that can be followed by something with which God will be prepared to coact."[30] In particular, Ockham says that "God antecedently wills everyone to be saved" and thus antecedently wills everyone to act so as to "persevere to the end."

> For He evidently gives [to everyone] antecedent conditions that can be followed by salvation, along with precepts and counsels to persevere to the end; and He will be prepared to coact with him, permitting him to will freely to act towards the attainment of salvation.[31]

But, as these passages show, in antecedently willing from eternity that a given created will should act in a certain way God does not determine the created will to act in that way. Accordingly, Ockham says:

> Now that these distinctions have been understood in this way, I say, along with others, that although nothing occurs contrary to the [consequent] disposing will of God, something may occur contrary either to the antecedent [disposing will] or to the revealed will of God . . . The second point—that something may occur contrary to the antecedent will of God—is proved as follows. For it is manifest that God gives everyone natural properties that can be followed by a meritorious act. And God is prepared to coact with everyone towards a meritorious act; nor will He show him the contrary—viz., His being unwilling that he should choose a meritorious act—for He will never command him [to do] the contrary. And He gives precepts

[30]*Ordinatio* I,d.46,q.1 C.
[31]*Ordinatio* I,d.46,q.1 G.

and counsels in order that he should follow through with a meritorious act. Nevertheless, not everyone chooses a meritorious act; many, indeed, choose demeritorious acts. The latter, therefore, act contrary to the antecedent divine will.[32]

Thus, although God's antecedent will regarding some future contingent may be settled by what is actual in the past, in such a way that there is no potency in things for Him to will the opposite, the proposition 'God antecedently willed that x will be A at *tm*' does not entail 'x will be A at *tm*'.

In his replies to Objections 3 and 3a in Question I of the *Treatise,* Ockham could, therefore, have agreed with the objector that Peter's predestination does involve a past action of God's will—viz., God's antecedently willing everyone to be saved. He would, however, disagree with the objector's claim that it is absurd to suppose that a past action of God could be obstructed by an act of a created will; for the action in question is an action of God's antecedent disposing will, which, as we have seen, may be obstructed in that way. In the replies he actually makes to Objections 3 and 3a, however, Ockham obviously takes the objector to be referring to the unobstructable consequent disposing will of God. Ockham grants the objector's premiss that if someone predestinate can be damned, he can be so only as a result of an act of a (his own) created will. What Ockham denies, however, is that it follows from this that the (consequent) divine will can be obstructed. The consequent divine will regarding Peter's predestination could be obstructed only if God's consequent will regarding Peter's predestination were settled in such a way that there was no potency in things for His willing the opposite, at a time when there was a double potency in things regarding Peter's eternal destiny—a potency for Peter's perseverance and supreme blessedness and a potency for his final impenitence and eternal damnation. But where the *consequent* will of God is concerned, 'God willed from eternity that Peter would receive supreme blessedness on the day of judgment' is *equivalent* to 'Peter will receive supreme blessedness on the day of judgment.' Consequently, it is not possible that the truth of the former be settled when the truth of the latter has yet to be settled by some future act of Peter's will, and not possible that the former be true when the latter is not true.

The position on which these replies are based, then, may be summarized as follows: (a) the *antecedent* disposing will of God regarding Peter's predestination is something settled by what is real

[32]*Ordinatio* I,d.46,q.1 D.

or actual in the past, in such a way that there is now no potency in things for the opposite, but something that can be obstructed by an act of Peter's will. (b) The *consequent* disposing will of God regarding Peter's will is something yet to be settled by what will be actual in the future—in particular, by Peter's actual choices—in such a way that before Peter's death there is still a potency in the way things are for God to will the opposite. But, as determined by Peter's choice, it cannot be obstructed by it or by anything else. In taking this position Ockham in effect denies that Peter's predestination is necessitated by any wholly past fact about God. In Assumption 1 Ockham explicitly rejects both this view and the view that predestination and reprobation are real relations. There he brings out his own view that neither 'predestination' nor 'reprobation' signifies anything really existing now or in the past except God and the person who will receive eternal blessedness or eternal punishment.

III. Is God's Knowledge of Future Contingents Certain and Infallible?

In Assumption 6, Ockham affirms,

> It must be held beyond question that God knows *with certainty* all future contingents—i.e., He knows with certainty which part of the contradiction is true and which false,[33]

but immediately acknowledges,

> It is difficult, however, to see *how* He knows this [with certainty], since one part [of the contradiction] is no more determined to truth than the other.[34]

The question is equally about divine psychology and the logical or metaphysical possibility of such knowledge. Both prove difficult for Ockham.

His predecessor, Duns Scotus, had not found them so. For he had held that God eternally has determinate knowledge of one part of a contradiction regarding future contingents, because He eternally wills one part to be true and the other to be false and His willing eternally settles it that one part rather than the other is determinately true.

Scotus's explanation may seem plausible at first. On the one hand, because God is omnipotent, 'God wills that Socrates will sit

---

[33] P. 48 below (italics added).
[34] Ibid.

down at *tm'* entails 'Socrates will sit down at *tm'*. Thus, it seems that God's willing one part of a contradiction to be true would suffice for His knowing that part to be true. On the other hand, because everything owes its existence and duration to God's creating and conserving it, nothing can come to be or continue to be unless God wills that it comes to be or continues to be. That is, 'Socrates will sit down at *tm'* entails 'God wills that Socrates will sit down at *tm.'* Thus, it might seem that for any pair of contradictories whatever, God wills one part rather than the other to be true. Therefore, God's willing one part rather than the other to be true would suffice to insure the certainty of God's determinate foreknowledge of one part of a contradiction in every case.

Scotus assumes that where propositions about the creation are concerned, God has a potency for willing the truth of *p* and a potency for willing the truth of not-*p* and that His eternally willing the truth of *p* eternally actualizes the former potency to the exclusion of the latter. Relying on his own understanding of the scope of the antecedent and consequent disposing will of God,[35] Ockham contends that Scotus's account cannot "preserve the certainty of God's knowledge in respect of future things that depend absolutely on a created will."[36]

To begin with, Ockham holds, it is the antecedent disposing will of God that is settled by what is actual from eternity. But where future things that depend absolutely on a created will are concerned, God's antecedent disposing will regarding them cannot insure the infallibility of His determinate cognition of them from eternity:

> For I ask whether or not the determination of a created will necessarily follows the determination of the divine will. If it does, then the will necessarily acts [as it does], just as fire does, and so merit and demerit are done away with. If it does not, then the determination of a created will is required for knowing determinately one or the other part of a contradiction regarding those [future things that depend absolutely on a created will]. For the determination of the created will does not suffice, because a created will can oppose the determination [of the uncreated will]. Therefore, since the determination of the [created] will was not from eternity, God did not receive certain cognition of the things that remained [for a created will to determine].[37]

For what the antecedent will eternally determines regarding acts of a created will is only (a) that every person should have certain

[35]See section II above.
[36]See Assumption 6, p. 49 below.
[37]P. 49 below.

natural properties—e.g., being a rational animal—and (b) that every person should be provided with precepts and counsels to guide him in his actions. Ockham assumes that the latter do not suffice to make the created will go one way rather than another. Consequently, if God's antecedent will determined a created will to act in a certain manner, this would be because (a) the natural properties thereby endowed determined the will so to choose, just as the nature of fire (or heat) determines fire to heat nearby combustible objects. In that case, the created will would be a natural cause that acted by natural necessity and hence not an appropriate subject of merit or demerit. And this is contrary to the doctrine that Ockham shares with Scotus—viz., that the will is a self-determining power for opposites.

It is only where the *consequent* disposing will of God is at issue that such propositions as 'God wills that Peter will deny Christ at *tm*' and 'Peter will deny Christ at *tm*' are equivalent. But that fact cannot help explain the eternal certainty of God's knowledge regarding future things that depend absolutely on a created will. For it follows from this equivalence that the consequent will of God regarding the truth of a future contingent proposition is just as contingent as is the truth of the proposition. Thus, even if God wills that Peter will deny Christ at *tm*' and 'Peter will deny Christ at *tm*' were—by (T8) and (T9)—determinately true from eternity, the exclusion of the potency in things for their determinate falsity had to await Peter's actual choice at *tm*. Ockham makes this very point regarding the (consequent) will of God in the second part of his critique of Scotus.

> Secondly, when something is determined contingently, so that it is still possible that it is not determined and it is possible that it was never determined, then one cannot have certain and infallible cognition based on such a determination. But the determination of the divine will in respect of future contingents is such a determination, both according to him [Scotus] and in truth. Therefore God cannot have certain cognition of future contingents based on such a determination.
>
> [The argument] is supported as follows. All such propositions as 'God from eternity willed this part of the contradiction to be true' and 'God from eternity determined this' are contingent, as is clear from Assumption 2. Consequently they can be true and [they can be] false. Therefore one will have no certain cognition based on such a determination.[38]

If the consequent disposing will of God regarding the truth of a future contingent proposition is just as contingent as is the truth

[38]Assumption 6, pp. 49–50 below.

of the proposition, then God's cognition of (or belief about) what His consequent will regarding such a proposition is, is no more and no less certainly correct than is His belief that the proposition is true.

According to Ockham, then, it is not by knowing something eternally actual that God eternally has certain and infallible knowledge of one part of a contradiction regarding future contingents. For he denies that anything that is eternally actual excludes the possibility of falsity (truth) for true (false) future contingent propositions. What alternative explanation can Ockham give of how God knows such propositions with certainty? He admits that 'it is impossible to express clearly the way in which God knows future contingents . . ." Nevertheless, foregoing silence, he suggests that

> . . . the following way [of knowing future contingents] can be ascribed [to God]. Just as the [human] intellect on the basis of one and the same [intuitive] cognition of certain non-complexes can have evident cognition of contradictory contingent propositions such as 'A exists' and "A does not exist', in the same way it can be granted that the divine essence is an intuitive cognition that is so perfect, so clear, that it is an evident cognition of all things past and future, so that it knows which part of a contradiction [involving such things] is true and which part false.[39]

Ockham recalls his own doctrine that in human knowledge, an intuitive cognition of Socrates is a cognition by virtue of which one has evident knowledge that Socrates exists when he exists, or evident knowledge that Socrates does not exist if he does not exist. An evident cognition is a cognition of a true proposition, a sufficient mediate or immediate cognition of which is an apprehension of its terms. If I have an intuitive cognition of Socrates, whether I am caused to judge that Socrates exists or that he does not exist depends on whether Socrates exists, is present, and acts together with the intuitive cognition to cause the former judgment in me. Since all possible particular creatures are objects of God's thought, Ockham is proposing to regard the divine act of understanding as an intuitive cognition of all of them and hence as an act by virtue of which God can have evident knowledge that they exist when they exist and that they do not exist when they do not exist. Unfortunately, the analogy falters at crucial points. Given the medieval doctrine of divine impassibility, no object ever causes anything in God. Further, our perfect intuitive cognitions cause evident judgments about the present only, whereas the

[39]Assumption 6, p.50.

puzzle is how God has certain and determinate knowledge regarding future contingents. Ockham does allow that we have imperfect intuitive cognitions which cause evident judgments about the past and even the future (*Reportatio* II,q.16; q.20 E). But the latter shed no light on how God knows future contingents with certainty, since Ockham offers no account of how we know on the basis of such premonitory cognitions either.

If Ockham is forced to plead ignorance of divine psychology, he must also face the charge that divine certainty and infallibility regarding future contingents is not even logically or metaphysically possible. For God could not have known from eternity that Peter would deny Christ at *tm* unless He judged from eternity that Peter would deny Christ at *tm*. Assuming that God's judgments are analogous to ours, for Him to judge that Peter would deny Christ at *tm* is for His act of understanding to be determinately directed in a certain way towards the proposition 'Peter will deny Christ at *tm*' rather than the proposition 'It is not the case that Peter will deny Christ at *tm*'. If so, given Ockham's position that temporal predicates apply nonmetaphorically to God, the proposition 'God judged from eternity that Peter would deny Christ at *tm*' was always a necessary proposition about the past. By contrast, 'Peter will deny Christ at *tm*' was a contingent proposition about the future for all times prior to *tm*, so that there was, for all that time, a possibility in things that God's eternal judgment should turn out to be false. Yet, if God were infallible regarding such propositions, it would be logically impossible for Him to be mistaken.

Ockham's response would be to insist on divine infallibility and compromise the analogy between divine and human judgment. For if God's judgments are all infallible, 'God judges that p is true' is expounded in part by 'p is true', just as much as 'God knows that p is true' is. Where p is a future contingent proposition, 'God judges (judged) that p is true' will also be a future contingent proposition, so far as its subject matter is concerned (*secundum rem*). But Ockham can sustain the latter claim only by denying that (T1) applies to divine judgments. Further, he would have to maintain the bizarre thesis that nothing real about the divine act of judgment, considered as it really is in itself, determines whether it is directed towards p or towards not-p instead. The latter move had already been made by Robert Grosseteste, but it leaves the intentionality of divine judgment utterly mysterious.

IV. Contingent and Immutable Truth
in Propositions about the Future

Another group of arguments in the *Treatise* attempts to raise problems for the doctrine that God has determinate knowledge of future contingents (Question II, Article II, Part One, (1), and Part Four) and the doctrine of predestination and reprobation (Question I, Objections 5, 5a, 6, 6a, and 7). In these arguments it is maintained that propositions about predestination and reprobation and propositions about God's knowledge cannot be true (or false) both contingently and immutably. This claim would, if true, pose difficulties for both doctrines.

The reasons for insisting on the *contingency* of such propositions have been reviewed in Parts I and II above. For, as Ockham and at least some of his objectors understand the doctrine of predestination and reprobation, it requires that a person's receiving supreme blessedness or eternal punishment on the day of judgment depends at least in part on that person's deliberation and free choice. But if ' "Peter is predestinate" is true at *tn*' entailed 'There is no potency in things after *tn* for "Peter is predestinate" to be false', then a person's (Peter's) deliberation would make no difference. Again, if the truth of propositions about God's determinate knowledge of future contingents were not something yet to be settled by what will be posited in actuality in the future, so that there is still a potency in things for the opposite, everything would happen of necessity and deliberation would be in vain. Thus it is Ockham's view that all such propositions are contingent.

The objectors, on the other hand, advance two sets of arguments to show that propositions about predestination and reprobation and propositions about God's knowledge must be *immutably* true (or false).

(i) Arguments of the first set depend on a principle that Ockham accepts—viz., that the assertion that someone is predestinate (or reprobate) *entails* the assertion that God will give supreme blessedness (or eternal punishment) to that person on the day of judgment. The reasoning is that if propositions such as 'Peter is predestinate' and 'Peter is reprobate' could change their truth-value, then 'Peter was predestinate at *t1*' and 'Peter is reprobate at *t2*' could be true at one and the same time (*t2*). But, by the principle cited above, 'Peter was predestinate at *t1*' and 'Peter is reprobate at *t2*' entail contradictory propositions (about the future) and therefore cannot both be true at once. Therefore, such propositions as 'Peter is predestinate' and 'Peter is reprobate' cannot change their truth-value, or are immutably true (or false).

(ii) Arguments of the second set rest on the claim that a change in the truth-value of a proposition about predestination or reprobation or in the truth-value of a proposition about God's knowledge would involve a change in God—i.e., in His will or in His knowledge, respectively. Any change in God is impossible, however; God is absolutely immutable. Therefore propositions about predestination or reprobation or propositions about God's knowledge cannot change their truth-value but are immutably true (or false). Ockham does not accept the claim on which these arguments rest and so rejects this second set of arguments.

The objectors' arguments that propositions about predestination or reprobation cannot be true (or false) *both* contingently and immutably are based on two closely related principles:

(T11) Every proposition that is true now and can be false can change from truth to falsity[40]

and

(T12) When opposites are related to each other in such a way that one cannot succeed the other, then if one of them is posited the other cannot be posited.[41]

For a proposition to *change* from truth to falsity as stipulated in (T11) it must first be settled by something posited in actuality that the proposition is true and at some later time be posited in actuality that the proposition is false. (The proposition 'The Empire State Building is gray,' for example, can change from truth to falsity. For if it is true now, its truth is settled by the actual inherence of gray color in the Empire State Building now; and if the Empire State Building is afterwards painted white, it will then be settled by what is posited in actuality that the proposition 'The Empire State Building is gray' is false.) (T11) is a corollary of the Aristotelian truth-theory, according to which the determinate truth (or falsity) of a proposition is invariably something settled by what is actual in the past or present. For when it is said in (T11) that a proposition can be false, what is meant is that there is still a

---

[40]Question I, Objection 5a, p.42 below.
[41]Question I, Objection 6, p, 42 below.

potency in things for the proposition to be false at a future time. According to Aristotelian truth-theory, if the proposition in question is true now, then its truth is settled by something posited in actuality in the past or present, in such a way that there is no longer any potency in things for its falsity. But contradictories cannot be posited in actuality at one and the same time. Therefore, on the Aristotelian truth-theory, if a proposition is true now and can be false, then the thing posited in actuality in the past or present that settles the truth of that proposition can at some future time cease to be posited in actuality, in which case the proposition can change from truth to falsity.

The two pairs of opposites to which principle (T12) is especially directed are, on the one hand, passive predestination and passive reprobation considered as real relations in the predestinate and reprobate, respectively and, on the other hand, active predestination and active reprobation considered as past or present acts of God's will.[42] For according to either of these views of predestination and reprobation, if Peter is predestinate now, then his predestination is settled by something posited in actuality in the past or present—i.e., either the form of predestination inhering in Peter now or God's past or present act of will. But, as noted in the arguments sketched above, whoever is predestinate is immutably predestinate, so that predestination and reprobation are opposites that cannot succeed each other. In that case the form of predestination cannot cease to inhere in Peter or the act of predestinating Peter cannot cease to be identical with the divine essence. Since contradictories cannot be posited in actuality in a single thing at one and the same time, the possibility no longer remains open that the form of reprobation should at some time inhere in Peter or that God should at some time will eternal punishment for Peter. Therefore, Peter cannot be predestinate but is rather necessarily predestinate, which is absurd.

Suppose, on the other hand, that one maintains that Peter, who is predestinate now, *can* nevertheless, *not* be predestinate. What this means, according to the two views of predestination cited above, is that even though the real form of predestination inheres in Peter now, the possibility still remains open that at some future time the form of predestination will not inhere in Peter (or that even though God now wills or has in the past willed supreme blessedness for Peter, the possibility remains open that at

[42]Theories 1 and 2, respectively, in Part II, pp. 12–16 above.

some future time God will not will supreme blessedness for Peter). But to allow either of these two possibilities is to allow that Peter can change from being predestinate to being reprobate, so that predestination and reprobation can succeed each other. (T12) would have a similar application to God's foreknowledge if one understood God's foreknowledge to be an act of cognition identical with the divine essence.

Ockham thinks the objectors are correct in deducing the consequences from (T11) and (T12). He agrees, for example, that "whatever is immutable and real is necessary."[43] Indeed, he uses just such entailments in his attempt to reduce to an absurdity the Aristotelian truth-theory and the "real relations" view of predestination and reprobation.[44] Ockham replies to the objectors not by raising quarrels over the putative consequences of (T11) and (12) but by denying the principles themselves,

He considers the rejection of (T11) so important that he devotes the whole of Question V to it, claiming to show there how future contingent propositions can be both immutably and contingently true (or false).

As for (T12), Ockham denies that it is true in general, since it does not have application to those opposites to which future contingents correspond. Ockham's rejection of the claim that predestination and reprobation are something real—either identical with the divine essence or in the persons predestinate or reprobate—has been discussed in Part II above, together with his arguments that 'Peter is predestinate' and 'God predestinated Peter' are equivalent to future contingent propositions. His claim that propositions about God's foreknowledge of future contingents are themselves future contingent propositions is discussed in Part I above.

V. The Contingency of Acts of Will

Scotus and Ockham agree that the will contrasts with natural causes in being or having a capacity for opposite objects or opposite acts. Both hold, too, that the will is naturally prior to its acts in that the acts depend for their existence on the existence and

[43]In his reply to Question I, Objection 5, p. 42 below.
[44]Question I, A, pp. 34–36 below and Assumption 2, pp. 45–46 below, respectively. (Boldface letters in our text correspond to marginal letters in Boehner's edition).

causal efficacy of the will, but not vice versa. And both concur in
(T1), that when the will acts, it actualizes its capacity for one object
or act to the exclusion of the other.

By contrast with fire, the will existing at a time before its
choice has a capacity for opposite objects or acts at some future
time: e.g., the will at $t1$ has a capacity for willing E at $t2$ and a
capacity for not willing E at $t2$. Likewise, the will willing E at $t2$ has
the capacity to continue to will E at $t3$ and a capacity to cease
willing E at $t3$. On this much, Scotus and Ockham are in accord.

So far, this account does not allow any contingency to the
divine will, which chooses eternally and immutably. Neither does
it allow that an angel could sin freely and contingently at the first
instant of his creation. Accordingly, Scotus argued that in addition
to the above-mentioned "evident" capacity for opposites, the will
has a "non-evident" capacity for opposites without succession. To
be sure, if the will is to choose contingently, it must be that the will
has a real capacity for opposites *prior* to the choosing. Nevertheless, Scotus observes that among things that exist at one and the
same time, some are naturally prior to others, so that within an
instant of time (or even the "now" of eternity) it is possible to
distinguish many instants of nature. Since the will and its
capacities are naturally prior to its acts, it is possible to remove the
contradiction apparent in the nonevident capacity for opposites by
relativizing the predications to instants of nature: 'The will has at
$(t1,n1)$ a real capacity for willing A at $t1$ and a real capacity for not
willing A at $t1$, and the will's real capacity for willing A at $t1$ is
actualized at $(t1,n2)$' is free from contradiction, although 'The will
has at $(t1,n1)$ a real capacity for willing A at $t1$ and a real capacity
for not willing A at $t1$, and the will's real capacity for willing A at
t1 is actualized at $(t1,n1)$' is not. Neither is 'The will wills A at
$(t1,n2)$ and the will does not will A at $(t1,n2)$'. Thus, although God
eternally and immutably wills whatever He wills, His volitions regarding creation are contingent, because at a prior instant of nature He eternally and immutably has a capacity for opposite
created objects; and an angel at the first instant of his creation
would have a capacity for opposite objects at an instant of nature
prior to that at which he actualizes one to the exclusion of the
other.

Scotus' solution of the theological puzzles about the divine
and angelic wills in terms of the "non-evident" capacity for opposites without (temporal) succession depends on his notion that "at
one and the same time, there is more than one instant of na-

ture."[45] But Ockham found the doctrine, with its ingenious attempt to justify the predication of contradictories about one and the same thing for one and the same time, entirely unacceptable. (a) In many passages, Ockham argues that there are no such instants of nature, because there are no things that such instants of nature could be. If there were, they would have to be either extramental or mind-dependent. Not the latter, because then "if there were no mind, nothing would be naturally prior—which is false."[46] If instants of nature were, extramental, they would have to be substances or accidents. Not accidents, because accidents exist in substances, not the reverse, whereas Socrates exists in an instant of nature prior to his volition. Not substances, because Socrates does not exist in an instant of nature in the way in which one substance exists in another extrinsic to it—e.g., water in a vase.

This frequently rehearsed attack seems doubly frivolous, however. First, Scotus never asserts that instants of nature are things (res) distinct from (other) substances and accidents. Second, relativizing predications to instants does not require instants to be things distinct from those that are said to exist in them. If it did, Ockham, who denies that instants of time are such distinct things, could not consistently relativize predications to instants of time.

(b) Ockham's sober objection to Scotus's instants of nature is that "it is proper to say that the prior exists *in something prior* in which the posterior did not exist,"[47] only where there is some measure of priority and posteriority. And Ockham contends that a measure is always really distinct from what is measured. The motions of heavenly bodies such as the sun provide such a really distinct measure of states of affairs. For example, we say that Moses' receiving of the law on Sinai occurred in an earlier period than the Babylonian captivity, because Moses' conversations with God coexisted with earlier and the Babylonian captivity with later revolutions of the sun. The prepositional phrase 'in an earlier period of time' signifies that the events are related to the successive revolutions in those ways. But Scotus cannot identify any such really distinct measure of natural priority and posteriority where God's eternal thoughts and volitions are concerned. For the natural priority of God's thought/volition of Himself over that of His

[45]*Treatise*, Question III B, p. 72.
[46]*Expositio in Librum Praedicamentorum Aristotelis*, c.18; OPh II, 328; *Ordinatio* I, d.9,q.3; OTh III. 304
[47]*Ordinatio* I,d.9,q.3; OTh III, 302.

thought/volition of others obtains eternally whether or not anything other than God exists, whereas no creature exists eternally.[48]

Ockham's discussion in Question III is difficult to follow, because he fails to make explicit his distinction between the antecedent and the consequent disposing will of God.[49] If this distinction is not taken into account, his position in Question III may seem inconsistent with his claims in Question I and the Assumptions regarding certain acts of the divine will. For in Question III Ockham maintains—apparently as regards any act of any will—that if x wills E at $t1$, it is not the case that at $t1$ x can *not* will E, nor is it the case that at $t2$ x can never have willed E at $t1$. In his discussion of predestination and reprobation earlier in the *Treatise*, however, Ockham maintains that such present-tense propositions as 'God wills supreme blessedness for Peter' are determinately true (or false) and yet can *not* be true and can *never* have been true. Ockham seems thereby to commit himself to the view—at least as regards such an act of the divine will—that there are instances of x's willing E at $t1$ in which at $t1$ x can *not* will E and at $t2$ x can *never* have willed E at $t1$. As an objector points out,[50] Ockham himself seems thus to have provided a counterexample to his position in Question III.

The objector's mistake would be apparent if Ockham had explicitly introduced his distinction between the antecedent and the consequent will into the *Treatise*. For it is only in the case of propositions regarding acts of God's antecedent disposing will that the determinate truth (or falsity) of past- and present-tense propositions is settled by what is posited in actuality—viz., by an act of will identical with the divine essence—in such a way that there is no potency in things for the opposite. The *consequent* disposing will of God regarding future contingents is *not* settled by what is actual in the past or present but has yet to be settled by what will be posited in actuality. Thus the truth (or falsity) of past- and present-tense propositions regarding acts of God's consequent disposing will in respect of future contingents—e.g., 'God has willed supreme blessedness for Peter,' 'God wills supreme blessedness for Peter'—has yet to be settled, and there is still a potency in things for their falsity (truth).

[48]Ibid.; OTh III, 303–4. *Expositio in Librum Praedicamentorum Aristotelis,*c.18; OPh II, 328.
[49]See Parts II and III of this Introduction.
[50]P. 73 below.

Ockham takes such propositions to be about God's consequent will when he maintains (in Question I and the Assumptions) that although true they can be false and can never have been true. His later conclusions (in Question III) regarding acts of the will apply to the will of God considered only as the antecedent disposing will, which is in all relevant respects like the human will.

VI. Can the Past Be Made Not to Have Been?

Our discussion above shows how (T1) lies at the root of many problems about the determinateness, certainty, and infallibility of divine foreknowledge, and the unobstructability of divine predestination. But (T1) had its medieval detractors—Gilbert of Poitiers and William of Auvergne in the thirteenth century and Thomas Buckhingham in the fourteenth—who denied the putative necessity of the past. Joining the medieval consensus that divine omnipotence does not include the power to make contradictories true, they went on to observe that 'Adam never existed' and 'Peter never denied Christ' are not contradictory. Further, God once had the power to make these propositions true—e.g., by deciding not to create Adam or Peter. And God's immutable power cannot be diminished by the passage of time or anything that happens among creatures.[51] Accordingly, they concluded that

> (T13) Even if 'x was A at tm' is true about the past, both as regards its wording and its subject matter, God has the power now (eternally) to bring it about that x was not A at tm, although He eternally never exercises that power.

Thus, even if Adam did exist, there is still a potency in things— viz., in God—for his never having existed; and even if Peter did deny Christ, there is still a potency in things—viz., in God—for his never having done so.

Their rejection of (T1) does not automatically rid them of the above problems about predestination, God's foreknowledge, and future contingents, however. For they have defended an exception to (T1) where divine power is concerned: whatever God wills, has willed, or shall will, He wills it in such a way that it is still (eternally) possible that He never have willed it. Like Scotus, they

[51]See Aquinas, *Summa Theologica* I, q.25,a.5, objection 2; and Gregory of Rimini, *Super Primum Sententiarum*, dd.42–44,q.1, f. 162rb–165ra.

thereby preserve the contingency of propositions about created world history—those about the past as much as those about the present and the future. But created free choice requires a real potency for opposites, not merely in God, but in the creature himself. And our questions have been whether the determinateness of God's knowledge (judgments) or choices is compatible with a real potency for opposites in the free creatures thereby known or destined. Even if a potency for opposites in God could coexist with God's determinate foreknowledge and choice that Peter deny Christ and yet not die in the sin of final impenitence, was there any potency for the opposite in Peter? And could a potency for the opposite in Peter survive Peter's actual denial? Further argument would be needed to show that (T1) admits of exceptions where created wills are concerned as well.

VII. "Causes" of Predestination and Reprobation

In Question IV, Ockham addresses himself, in cryptic fashion, to the thorny question of God's motives in predestinating some and reprobating others. Certain statements in the Gospels and Epistles seem to commit Christians to

(T14) From eternity, God immutably chose some rational creatures (the elect) to order to eternal life (to predestine) and rejected others, thereby abandoning them to eternal punishment.

But is there anything about the particular creatures that explains God's actual choice? Some—e.g,, Aquinas—argued that there could not be: since God is free and sovereign, He can accept or predestine (reject or reprobate) whomever He likes. His two-fold goodness requires only that there be some of each: the predestinate to show forth His mercy and the reprobate His justice (*Summa Theologica* I,q.23, a.5 c and ad 3um). Others—e.g., Henry of Ghent—contended that in view of the high stakes for creatures—eternal life versus eternal punishment—as well as the Scriptural assertion that

(T15) God does not play favorites,

it must be that God bases His decision on foreseen free choices of the creatures themselves (*Quodlibeta* VIII,q.5; 1518 ed.). Yet, grace must play some role, if the Pelagian heresy is to be avoided.

In his own solution, Ockham tries to give full weight to divine grace, freedom, and sovereignty, while assigning created free choice a criterial role. So far as God's actual redemptive plan is concerned, Ockham agrees with Augustine that "God is not a punisher before man is a sinner," and in *Ordinatio* I, d.40, q.u, assumes that "eternal life is conferred on an adult only because of some meritorious deed, while "no one is condemned to perpetual punishment—i.e., sensory punishment—except by reason of his own demerit."[52] To escape the snares of Pelagianism, he invokes his own unique value-theory, according to which

(T16) "God is in no way a debtor to anyone."[53]

(T15) is its trivial consequence: for "it can be said that He plays favorites, only when the persons are equal and something is owed to each and conferred on one and not the other,"[54] But God owes nothing to any created person—in particular, neither eternal life nor eternal punishment. Again, it follows that

(T17) No creature is such that it is necessarily or intrinsically acceptable (unacceptable) to God; none such that is necessarily or intrinsically worthy of eternal life (eternal punishment).[55]

Although creatures do have natural goodness or privations prior to and independently of divine acceptance or rejection, the properties of being worthy of eternal life or eternal punishment are not to be identified with any of them. Rather they are created by divine free choices to count this person worthy of eternal life (eternal punishment) under certain conditions, the way the commercial value of coins or paper money is created by government laws and the semantic properties of marks and sounds by the contingent habits of language-users. That there is any plan of salvation at all, and that it assigns eternal life to obedient free choices and eternal punishment to ultimate and unrepentent sinning, is a matter of divine free choice, which could have turned in another direction.

In Question IV, Ockham acknowledges that his general ac-

[52]*Reportatio* III, q.5 L, N; IV, q. 3 F.
[53]OTh IV,593–4.
[54]*Ordinatio* I,d.41,q.7; OTh IV, 608.
[55]Asserted regarding acceptance or worthiness of eternal life: *Ordinatio* I,d.17,q.1; OTh III, 446, 449, 452, 454–5; d.17,q.2; OTh III, 471–2; *Reportatio* III, q.5 0; *Reportatio* IV, q.3 Q. Regarding God's hating a creaturae: *Ordinatio* I,d.17,q.1; OTh III, 447, 449. Regarding a deed or person being worthy of eternal punishment: *Reportatio* IV, q.3 F.

count of God's motives admits of apparent counter-examples. Most obvious are the baptized and unbaptized infants who die before they reach the age of reason. Here Ockham follows a popular line that God's reasons for predestinating the former and condemning the latter lie in the free choices, not of the infants, but of the adults who do or do not bring them to the sacrament. And he adds that such infants suffer a milder penalty than adults who are condemned for their own sinful free choices.

Of special importance for Ockham was the case of the Blessed Virgin. Surely God would have found the idea of Christ's mother suffering eternal punishment entirely unacceptable. Yet, God would be forced to accept that risk, given (T5) and a general policy of predestinating adults only on the basis of the person's own free choices.

In Question IV, Ockham reasons that either the Blessed Virgin and the good angels actually did choose in such a way as to merit eternal happiness, given existing divine ordinances, or they did not. If they persevered to the end and did not commit the sin of final impenitence, then the general policy of predestination on the basis of foreseen free choices does not admit of an exception in their case. On the other hand, if they did not persevere, the policy does admit of exceptions.

Facing the same difficulty in *Ordinatio* I,d.41, q.u, Ockham seems unwilling to countenance the idea that the Blessed Virgin actually sinned, and so concludes that

> "some will be saved because of their merits in such a way that if they had not voluntarily earned merit, they would not be saved. Some, however, are ordered to eternal life by a special grace, in such a way that they are not left on their own the way others are, but are prevented from putting any obstacle [to their having] and are prevented from losing eternal life. This is the way it was, for example, with the Blessed Virgin and certain others: divine grace prevented them from sinning and losing eternal life."[56]

In the former case, the foreseen created free choice is God's reason for predestination, but in the second

> there seems to be no reason why they are predestinated except that God wills it, so that whatever He gives them, He gives them in order that eternal life may follow, and He does not permit anything in them that could be an obstacle to eternal life.[57]

[56]*Ordinatio* I,d.41,q.4; OTh IV, 606.
[57]Ibid., 607.

God takes no risk that the Blessed Virgin might commit sin, because He prevents her by certain grace. Yet, if so, how is she free?

Ockham struggles with this problem in *Reportatio* III,q.2. His first thought is that God insures her impeccability with respect to sins of *commission* by regularly cooperating with her to produce good or virtuous acts and withdrawing His cooperation from bad or vicious acts. Since without divine cooperation, no act exists, the Blessed Virgin will never perform any sinful acts. She is free to will or not to will a good act, but she is not free to elicit a bad act.[58] Nevertheless, she can act meritoriously, because she is free to choose from a variety of good acts.[59]

Preserving her from sins of *omission* is more difficult. For it seems that if the Blessed Virgin ceased to elicit a good act that she was obliged to perform, she omits to fulfill one of her obligations. Ockham's first response is that she would never have been without any act to which she was obligated; for had she ever ceased to produce it, God would have acted alone to preserve that act in existence. This answer seems inadequate, however. For a sin of omission is not avoided by the mere presence of the act in the agent. For if God acts alone to continue an act that the Blessed Virgin was obliged to continue but did not, she has still abdicated her responsibility to be a partial efficient cause of the continuance of that act.

In the end, Ockham appeals to his divine-command theory of obligation, according to which a creature's obligations are entirely a matter of divine choice. God could preserve the Blessed Virgin's impeccability in ceasing to produce the act simply by ordaining that she does not sin if she does not elicit the act,[60] or He may have ordained that "when she elicited a good act, she earned merit, but when not, then He ordained that she was not obliged to act meritoriously."[61]

Nevertheless, it may be objected that Ockham's account— according to which God preserves the impeccability of the Blessed Virgin and select others by making exceptions to His general policy—runs afoul of (T15). When God loves Jacob and hates Esau, blesses Mary and curses Judas, is He not exhibiting unjust favoritism? Ockham will repeat that God commits no injustice, because creatures have no rights against God for Him to violate.

---

[58]*Reportatio* III, q.2 C.
[59]*Reportatio* III, q.2 D.
[60]*Reportatio* III, q.2 E.
[61]*Reportatio* III, q,2 F,

Neither Mary nor Judas has any right to receive eternal life or to avoid eternal punishment.

Yet, if God is not thus unjust, is this arbitrariness not a mark against His wisdom? Ockham will insist that it is not. For God is not said to be wise because His choices measure up to some standards of moral appropriateness independent of His will. Rather He is wise in that He is rational in pursuing His purposes, skilled in selecting the means to His chosen ends. Whether or not He is rational in treating like cases differently depends upon whether or not it suits His purposes. Even from a human point of view, we can understand a reason for wanting to guarantee the Mother of Christ a place in His heavenly kingdom. And if His eternal selection of Mary instead of Elizabeth to be the Mother of Christ were, like His election of Jacob over Esau, arbitrary, this fact would not keep it from being a manifestation of divine wisdom. In the end, Ockham could insist that if it is at times not irrational or foolish for us to do something simply because we want to, how much less so for God!

—MARILYN McCORD ADAMS

PREDESTINATION, GOD'S FOREKNOWLEDGE, AND FUTURE CONTINGENTS

[QUESTION I][1]

A   Regarding the subject of predestination and foreknowledge, it should be observed that those[2] who suppose that passive predestination and passive foreknowledge are real relations in the

[1]Square brackets enclose words or phrases introduced into the text by the translators. An asterisk following a word (as on p. 36) indicates that we are adopting one of the variant readings cited in the footnotes to Boehner's edition. The contents of Ockham's treatise are organized around the consideration of five questions, all but the first of which are explicit in the text. Question I might be worded 'Are passive predestination and passive foreknowledge real relations in the person who is predestinate and foreknown?' Ockham first produces an argument in support of a negative answer to this question and then deals with a series of objections to the argument or the answer. In Boehner's edition of the treatise the heading "[*Quaestio Prima seu Dubium Primum*]" is not supplied until the point at which marginal letter B appears. In his article "Ockham's *Tractatus de Praedestinatione et de Praescientia Dei et de Futuris Contingentibus* and its Main Problems" (in Philotheus Boehner, *Collected Articles on Ockham*, ed. Eligius M. Buytaert, "Franciscan Institute Publications, Philosophy Series" No. 12; St. Bonaventure, N.Y., The Franciscan Institute, 1958; pp. 420–441) Boehner is accordingly led to the mistaken view that Question I is concerned to show that "Even he who is opposed to real distinct relations has to admit contradictory propositions" (p. 422). In the manuscripts on which Boehner's edition is based the only occurrence of the heading "*Quaestio Prima*" is here at the beginning of the treatise.

[2]One of those Ockham is referring to may be Alexander of Hales (d. 1275), who

34

[person who is] predestinate and foreknown have necessarily to admit contradictories.[3]

Proof of the claim: I take someone — A — who is now predestinate, and I ask whether or not A can commit the sin of final impenitence.[4]

If he cannot, then necessarily he will be saved, which is absurd.

If he can, then suppose that he does commit [that] sin. On this supposition 'A is reprobate' is true.[5] And then I ask whether or not the real relation of predestination has been destroyed.

If it has not been destroyed, then it remains in A when A is reprobate. Consequently A will be at one and the same time both reprobate and predestinate, since if such a relation is a relation really existing in A, A can be denominated by it.[6]

If it is destroyed, then at any rate it will always be true to say

---

held the view that predestination (or reprobation) is a form really inhering in the predestinate (or reprobate) person. Alexander thought, moreover, that the inherence of the form of predestination (or reprobation) in someone "settled it" that that person would receive eternal life (or eternal punishment) on the day of judgment. Thus 'A is predestinate' would entail 'A will receive eternal life' and 'B is reprobate' would entail 'B will receive eternal punishment.' See Alexander's *Summa theologica*, Pars I, Inq. I, Tract. V, Sect. II, Quaest. IV, Tit. 1, c. iii, 233, where he seems, evidently mistakenly, to ascribe this view to Peter Lombard (d. 1160/64), the author of the *Sentences*.

[3]Compare the similar argument in Book One of Ockham's *Commentary on the Sentences* (the *Ordinatio*), d. 30, q. 2, C; also his *Summa logicae*, III (3), c. 31 (edn. Venet., 1508, fol. 90ra). (Boehner) (The data in references followed by Boehner's name in parentheses are supplied in the notes to his edition of the *Treatise*.) To suppose that passive predestination — i.e., the condition of being predestinate — is a real relation in the predestinate person is to suppose that it is on a par with, say, the real relation of filiation in a child. For Ockham's opponents, a real relation was not only one that obtains independently of any mental act, but a thing (*res*) really distinct from substance and quality.

[4]A person is said to commit the sin of final impenitence when he dies without having confessed or repented of some mortal sin he has committed.

[5]Ockham's reasoning is governed by the doctrine that predestination and reprobation are jointly exhaustive as well as mutually exclusive conditions for all human beings.

[6]I.e., passive predestination and passive reprobation can be ascribed to or predicated of A. Cf. Ockham's *Summulae in libros Physicorum* III, c. 15: "In the broad sense '*denominatio*' is used for '*praedicatio*.' '*Denominatio*' is taken strictly when a denominative name [such as 'predestinate'] signifying two things (one directly and the other, inhering in the first, indirectly) . . . is predicated of something." On denominative names (or paronyms) generally see Aristotle, *Categories*, Ch. 8 (10a27–10b12), and Desmond Paul Henry, *The De Grammatico of St. Anselm: The Theory of Paronymy*, University of Notre Dame Medieval Studies, Vol. XVIII; Notre Dame, Ind., University of Notre Dame Press, 1965.

afterwards that there was such a relation in *A*, since according to the Philosopher in Book VI of the *Ethics* [Ch. 2, 1139b10-11], "in this alone is God deprived: to make undone things that have been done." (This is to be understood in the following way. If some assertoric proposition[7] merely about the present that is not equivalent to one about the future is true now, so that it is true of the present, then it will always be true of the past.[8] For if the proposition 'this thing is' — some thing or other having been indicated — is true now, then 'this thing was' will be true forever after, nor can God in His absolute power[9] bring it about that this proposition be false.) Therefore, since 'this relation is in *A*' was true at some time, 'this relation was in *A*' will always be true. Therefore '*A* was predestinate' will* always be true, nor can it be false as the result of any power whatever. And then this follows further: he is reprobate now; therefore 'he was reprobate' will always be true after this instant. Thus at one and the same instant '*A* was predestinate' and '*A* was reprobate' will be true. Further, he was therefore predestinate and not predestinate, reprobate and not reprobate.

There is no way in which this argument can be resolved as long as one supposes that predestination and foreknowledge are real relations.

B   There are, nevertheless, some objections to what has been said so far.

[Objection]1. The conclusion seems to be opposed as much to those who deny as to those who suppose [that they are real] relations. For I take someone existing [in a state of] charity[10] — the same is

---

[7] Reading '*de inesse mere*' for '*mere de inesse.*' Ockham, *Summa logicae* II, c. 1: "An assertoric proposition (*propositio de inesse*) is one without a mode . . . [the four principal modes being] necessary, impossible, contingent, and possible."

[8] As is shown by the examples in the next sentence, this is stated oversimply. Ockham ordinarily claims in this treatise, and evidently means to claim here, that such a proposition about the present *has corresponding to it* a proposition about the past such that if the first is true now the second will be true forever after.

[9] Viewed as *absolute*, God's power is His ability to act in any way not involving a contradiction. God's acting in accordance with the laws He has freely established is described as the exercise of His *ordered* power. Ockham discusses this distinction in *Quodlibeta* VI, q. 1, and in *Summa logicae* III (4), c. 6.

[10] Ockham, *Quodlibeta* VI, q. 1: "['*Caritas*'] is taken in one way for a quality of the soul [the quality commonly known as 'Christian charity'], in another way for divine acceptance." Cf. Leon Baudry, *Lexique Philosophique de Guillaume d'Ockham* (Paris, P. Lethielleux, 1958), art. "*Caritas*": ". . . a man can be acceptable to God from the standpoint of absolute power without *caritas* in the first sense of the word; [without *caritas*] in the second sense, he cannot."

predestinate—and then I ask whether or not charity can be destroyed; and the conclusion deduced earlier follows whether it can or cannot be destroyed.[11]

[Reply.] I maintain that what he assumes is false, for 'everyone existing [in a state of] charity is predestinate' is false, just as 'everyone who commits mortal sin is reprobate' is false. For Peter and Paul committed mortal sin but were never reprobate; similarly, Judas sometimes performed a meritorious act[12] *(meruit)* but was not then predestinate. For these propositions [viz., 'everyone existing in a state of charity is predestinate' and 'everyone who commits mortal sin is reprobate'] are equivalent to some about the future, since they are equivalent [respectively] to these: 'God will give these [existing in a state of charity] eternal life' and 'God will give those [having committed mortal sin] eternal punishment.' [But corresponding propositions about the future—viz., 'God will give Peter eternal life' and 'God will give Peter eternal punishment'] do not follow [respectively] from 'Peter is in [a state of] charity' and 'Peter has committed mortal sin.'[13] Therefore, if no one could be in [a state of] charity without having been predestinate, the conclusion of the argument would be opposed as much to those who deny as to those

---

[11]Note that the "I" of this paragraph is not Ockham but an objector. Objection 1, unlike the other objections in Question 1, is a direct criticism of the argument Ockham has just offered. It evidently rests on the claim that whether or not passive predestination is a real relation in the predestinate, charity is a quality really distinct from and inhering in the person who is in a state of charity. The objector assumes not only the commonly accepted thesis that if *x* is in a state of charity, *x* is accepted by God, but also that '*x* is in a state of charity' entails '*x* is predestinate'. Ockham follows the theological consensus when he rejects the latter entailment.

[12]Baudry, *Lexique,* art. *"Meritum"*: ". . . As far as we know, Ockham nowhere presented a formula that summarized his entire doctrine of merit. But since he defends Duns Scotus's views against Peter Auriol, the following definition, propounded by Duns Scotus, may perhaps be presented as expressive of his thought: A meritorious act is the act of a free will produced under the influence of grace and accepted by God as worthy of supreme blessedness. . . ." If this definition *is* expressive of Ockham's thought, then God's acceptance of an *act* as worthy of supreme blessedness is not tantamount to his predestinating the *agent* of that act. In this reply Ockham obviously does take it for granted that if one performs a meritorious act one is in a state of divine acceptance, even if only temporarily.

[13]The position Ockham takes in opposition to the view that passive predestination is a real relation, and on which he bases this reply, is stated in Assumptions 1–4, of which Assumption 4 is especially pertinent here. Ockham's reply is complicated at this point by an unnecessary shift from a plural to a singular example.

who suppose [that they are real] relations. But that is false, and so
the conclusion is not [of that sort].

C   [Objection] 2. Every proposition about the present that is
true at some time has [corresponding to it] a necessary[14] proposition about the past. For example, if 'Socrates is seated' is true, 'Socrates was seated' will be necessary forever after. But suppose 'Peter
is predestinate' is now true; in that case 'Peter was predestinate' will
always be necessary. Then I ask whether or not he can be damned.
If he can be so, suppose that he is. Then 'Peter is reprobate' is true
of the present; therefore 'Peter was reprobate' will always be necessary of the past. Thus 'Peter was predestinate' and 'Peter was reprobate' would be true at one and the same time.

[Reply.] I maintain that the major premiss is false (as is clear
from Assumption 3 [pp. 46–47 below]); for that proposition that is
about the present in such a way that it is nevertheless equivalent to
one about the future and its truth depends on the truth of the one
about the future does not have [corresponding to it] a necessary
proposition about the past. On the contrary, the one about the past
is contingent, just as is its [corresponding proposition] about the
present.[15] All propositions having to do with predestination and
reprobabion are of this sort (as is clear from Assumption 4 [p.
47 below]), since they all are equivalently about the future even
when they are verbally (*vocaliter*) about the present or about the
past.[16] Therefore 'Peter was predestinate' is contingent just as is
'Peter is predestinate.'

And when you ask whether Peter can be damned, I reply that

[14]In the terminology of at least one thirteenth-century logician, William of
Sherwood, such a proposition is "necessary *per accidens*" and not to be confused with
propositions "necessary *per se*": ". . . in case something cannot be false now or in the
future or in the past it is said to be 'necessary *per se*' – e.g., 'God is.' But it is 'necessary
per accidens' in case something cannot be false now or in the future although it could
have been [false] in the past – e.g., 'I have walked' " (in Norman Kretzmann, *William
of Sherwood's Introduction to Logic*, Minneapolis, University of Minnesota Press, 1966.
p. 41). See Introduction, pp. 5–9 above. In at least one place (*Ordinatio*, Prologus, q.
6) Ockham himself uses the label "necessary *per accidens*." He says, "Many propositions about the past are of this sort. They are necessary *per accidens* because it was
contingent that they would be necessary, and they were not always necessary."
[15]For a discussion of the basis of this objection see Introduction, pp. 5–9 above.
For the basis of Ockham's reply, see Introduction, pp. 12–16.
[16]The frequently recurring phrase "all propositions having to do with predestination and reprobation" (our rendering of the even vaguer Latin "*omnes proposi-
tiones in ista materia*") is intended to cover primarily propositions (*a*) in which passive

he can be so and that we can suppose that he is. In that case, however, 'Peter is reprobate and Peter was predestinate' will be false, since if one of a pair of contradictories is posited—i.e., if it is posited that it is true—the other will be false. But 'Peter was predestinate' and 'Peter was reprobate' include contradictories—viz., 'God will give eternal life to Peter' and 'God will not give eternal life to Peter.'[17] Therefore if one is true the other is false, and vice versa.

D   [Objection] 3. If someone predestinate can be damned, [he can be so] only as a result of an act of a created will. Conse-

---

predestination or passive reprobation is predicated of some person or (*b*) in which God is said to predestinate or reprobate some person. Propositions of type (*a*) and of type (*b*) are discussed in present-tense and in past-tense versions. Where present-tense versions alone are at issue, Ockham is likely to say that such a proposition "is equivalent to one about the future" (see, e.g., pp. 36, 37, 38). Thus, for example, it is part of Ockham's view that 'Peter is predestinate' is equivalent to 'Peter will receive eternal life.' His treatment of past-tense versions is, however, more problematic. Where they are at issue, either alone or together with present-tense versions, he is likely to say not that such a proposition is equivalent to one about the future but rather that it is "equivalently about the future" (see, e.g., p. 47). One reason for the apparent ambivalence of this claim may be the difficulty regarding the status of such a proposition after the time of the granting of eternal life. On the one hand it seems clear that after that time 'Peter will receive eternal life' is false (see p. 62) and 'Peter is predestinate' is likewise false, even though both were true before that time. On the other hand there is at least an understandable tendency to say that 'Peter was predestinate' continues to be true after that time, and this may account for the apparent ambivalence of the claim regarding its logical relation to 'Peter will receive eternal life.' One reason why Ockham rejects the "real relations" view is that he rejects the notion that there is any event in the past that can be correctly described as the occasion of Peter's predestination, or that there is anything actual in the past that settles it that Peter will receive eternal life on the day of judgment, or that there is any temporally persisting real condition in Peter that can be correctly described as Peter's status as a predestinate person. Consequently, Ockham *would* want to deny that 'Peter was predestinate' remains true after the time of the granting of eternal life, but he seems never to have come to the point of doing so explicitly. Perhaps he ought to have disallowed or at least cautioned against such past-tense versions as 'Peter was predestinate' and (more especially) 'God predestinated Peter' as at best misleading on his view. At any event his treatment of them will be less confusing if one reads all of it as conducted under the condition he states explicitly near the end of the *Treatise* (p. 79): ". . . with the understanding that the proposition . . . is under consideration only prior to the granting of supreme blessedness."

[17]As was pointed out in note 16, Ockham almost certainly does want to claim that the first and second of these propositions *are equivalent to* the third and fourth, respectively. Still, it is worth noting that he here makes what appears to be a weaker claim—viz., that the first and second *include* (evidently *entail*) the third and fourth, respectively—and that even that claim is most easily accepted under the condition mentioned at the end of note 16.

quently an act of the divine will can be obstructed by such an act [—which is absurd].[18]

[Reply.] I grant the premiss, but I reject the inference. An act of the divine will is not obstructed by an act of a created will, unless something opposed to a standing divine ordinance were to occur as a result of some other will, in which case 'God has predestinated Peter' and 'Peter is damned as a result of an act of his own will' would be true at one and the same time. But they cannot hold good (*stare*) at one and the same time, since if 'Peter is damned because of an evil act of his own will' is true, then 'Peter is predestinate' was never true. Similarly, if 'Peter is damned' is true, then 'Peter was preordained to eternal life' was never true.

[Objection 3a.] The argument is supported in the following way. Suppose God has determined Peter to be saved. I ask whether or not in that case Peter's will would follow necessarily the determination of the divine will. If not, the divine will is obstructed. If so, the thesis [that someone predestinate cannot be damned] is established.

[Reply.] I maintain that a created will follows a divine ordinance or determination not necessarily but freely and contingently. But it does not follow further from the previously stated argument that the divine will can be obstructed, since the truth of 'God predestinated Peter' is inconsistent with (*non potest stare cum*) the truth of 'Peter is damned.'[19]

E   [Objection] 4. The proposition 'God predestinated Peter' was true from eternity. Therefore it cannot be false. Therefore it is necessary.[20]

[Reply.] I reject the inference, since many propositions were true from eternity that are false now. For example, 'the world does not exist' was true from eternity and nevertheless is false now. Thus I maintain that even if 'God predestinated Peter' will have been true from eternity, it can nevertheless be false and it can fail ever to have been true.

---

[18]In his *Opus Oxoniense* (I, d. 40, q. u., n. 1, arg. 2 (Boehner)), Duns Scotus addresses himself to this argument expressed in these same words. Ockham's reply is, however, quite different from Scotus's in its strategy.

[19]See Assumption 6. See also Introduction, pp. 17–20 above, on the antecedent and the consequent disposing will of God.

[20]Objection 4 bears some resemblance to Aristotle's argument in *De caelo* I, Ch. 12, 281b20–25, which concludes "therefore everything that exists forever is absolutely indestructible."

F   [Objection] 5. Since everything that is God or is in God is necessary, divine predestination is necessary.[21] Therefore, necessarily He predestinated Peter. Therefore Peter necessarily is predestinate, and so not contingently.

[Reply.] I maintain that 'predestination is necessary' can be understood in two different ways. In one way [it can be understood as the claim] that that which is principally signified by the noun 'predestination' is necessary. [Understood] in this way, I grant it, since that [which is principally signified] is the divine essence, which is necessary and immutable. In another way [it can be understood as the claim that that which is secondarily signified by the noun 'predestination' — viz.,] that someone is predestinated by God [— is necessary]. [Understood] in this way, [predestination] is not necessary, for just as everyone who is predestinate,* contingently is predestinate, so God contingently predestinates everyone [who is predestinate].[22]

And when it is said that divine predestination is immutable and therefore absolutely necessary, I maintain that what is immutable and real is necessary.[23] When, however, we are speaking of an immutable complex[24] — ['mutable' and 'immutable'] in the sense in which one complex can change from truth to falsity and vice versa and another complex cannot change in that way — then not everything immutable is necessary. For there is some contingent proposition that cannot be first true and afterwards false and vice versa, so that it is [not] true to say of it 'this proposition is true now but was false earlier' and vice versa, and yet [this proposition] is not

[21]Objection 5 is evidently based on the "real relations" view of *active* predestination, considering it to be a condition really inhering in God and hence necessary. The basis of Ockham's reply is his general denial of the "real relations" view. Active predestination is no more a real relation in God than is passive predestination in Peter, and to speak of God's predestination of Peter is simply to speak of God's granting eternal life to Peter at some future time.

[22]Compare the account of the signification of 'predestination' in Assumption 1 with the account presented in this reply. The difference between the two accounts is partly the result of the fact that it is really the signification only of '*divine* (or *active*) predestination' that is presented here. This account is more easily followed if one thinks of it as applied to the analysis of 'divine predestination' — viz., 'God's granting eternal life to someone at some future time' — which signifies *principally* God Himself, the agent, and *secondarily* His future action.

[23]Cf. Book One of Ockham's *Commentary on the Sentences* (the *Ordinatio*), d. 40, q. 1, **B** (Boehner). Notice that the first clause of this sentence introduces a variation on Objection 5 and that Ockham's reply to it begins in the second clause and continues through the remainder of the paragraph.

[24]A "complex" here is a complex of terms — i.e., a proposition.

necessary but contingent. The reason for this is that although* by hypothesis [the proposition] is true and will have been true, it is nevertheless possible that it is not true and that it will never have been absolutely true. For example, 'God knows that this person will be saved' is true and yet is possible that He will never have known that this person will be saved. And so that proposition is immutable and is nevertheless not necessary but contingent.[25]

[Objection 5a.] On the contrary: every proposition that is true now and can be false can change from truth to falsity. But suppose that the proposition 'Peter is predestinate' is true now and can be false (as is* consistent); therefore ['Peter is predestinate' can change from truth to falsity].[26]

[Reply.] I maintain that the major premise is false, since more is required — i.e., that the proposition that will be false or will be capable of being false was true at some time. Therefore, although the proposition 'Peter is predestinate' is true now and can be false, nevertheless when it will be false, it will* be true to say that it never was true. Therefore it cannot change from truth to falsity.

G   [Objection] 6. When opposites are related to each other in such a way that the one cannot succeed the other, then if one of them is posited the other cannot be posited — as is clear regarding blindness and vision. But to be predestinate and to be damned are [opposites] of this kind. Therefore [if one of them is posited the other cannot be posited].

[Reply.] I maintain that this is not true as regards such opposites as those to which future contingents correspond — opposites such as to be predestinate and to be reprobate. Therefore, although they could not succeed each other, still it does not follow that if one obtains the other cannot obtain.[27]

---

[25]In this reply Ockham presents the first sketch of the main line of his position, which is retraced in greater detail in, e.g., Question II, Article III, Part One, and Question V. See Introduction, pp. 26–30 above.

[26]Here as elsewhere in the remainder of the *Treatise* the conclusion is left unexpressed, the argument ending with the formula "*igitur, etc.*" In every such case we supply the intended conclusion within brackets.

[27]The objector's example is open to misinterpretation unless it is understood that the blindness is absolutely incurable. The fact that incurable blindness can succeed vision while vision cannot succeed incurable blindness is of no consequence to the objection or to Ockham's reply, even though in the case of predestination and reprobation neither can succeed the other. The reply rejects the objector's analogy solely because blindness is a real condition and hence subject to necessity *per accidens* (see note 14). Peter's blindness is a condition that is posited in actuality; Peter's pre-

[Objection 6a.] On the contrary: concerning everyone of whom it is true to say today that he is predestinate and nevertheless that he can be reprobate tomorrow, 'predestinate' and 'reprobate' can be successively verified of[28] him. Therefore [these opposites can succeed each other].

[Reply.] I deny it, unless it could be truly said when he is reprobate that he was at some time predestinate. Therefore, since this cannot be said in the case put forward, they are not successively verified of one and the same person, nor can they be.

H   [Objection] 7. One whom God predestinated from eternity He cannot not predestinate, for otherwise He could change [−which is absurd]. Therefore if God predestinated Peter from eternity, then from eternity He cannot not predestinate him. As a consequence, necessarily he will be saved.

[Reply.] I maintain that the first proposition is false, since all such [propositions] as 'God predestinated Peter from eternity' and 'Peter was predestinated from eternity' are contingent, since they can be true and they can be false − not *successively*, however, so that they are true after they were false, or vice versa. Therefore, even though 'God predestinated Peter from eternity' and [other propositions] of that kind are true now, before Peter is granted supreme blessedness, they can nevertheless be false. If he should in fact be damned, then [that proposition] is false in fact (or [such propositions] are false in fact). [Such propositions,] therefore, are just as contingent with the phrase 'from eternity' as without it. Nor do they present any difficulty other than that presented by those that are verbally about the present.[29]

---

destination, on the other hand, has not been posited in actuality and will not be posited in actality (if at all) until the day of judgment. If 'Peter is blind' is true now, then 'Peter sees' cannot be true now (or at any subsequent time). But to say that 'Peter is predestinate' is true now is to say only that 'Peter will receive eternal life' is true now. Ockham acknowledges that there cannot be a subsequent time at which that ceases to be true and 'Peter will receive eternal punishment' begins to be true, but in the absence of a past or present real condition in Peter determining a necessity *per accidens* he sees no reason to deny that 'Peter will receive eternal punishment' *can* be true even though 'Peter will receive eternal life' *is* true.

[28]Here, as elsewhere in the *Treatise*, 'verified of' means 'used as predicate terms in true, affirmative, present-tense propositions about.'

[29]Ockham's denial of any special force to the phrase 'from eternity' seems justified, but (for reasons given in note 16) it is not so easy to accept his claim that past-tense propositions present no special difficulty. (In connection with the discussion in note 16 it is worth noting that he does here explicitly introduce the condition 'before Peter is granted supreme blessedness.')

J   [Objection] 8.[30] I ask regarding the things that have been revealed by the Prophets whether or not necessarily they come to pass as they have been revealed. If so, then since such things are future, it follows that their opposite cannot come to pass. On the other hand, if not, then 'this is revealed'—where some such thing is indicated—was true at some time and therefore was ever afterwards necessary. Now it was not revealed as false, for the Prophets did not say what is false. Therefore it was revealed as true. Therefore it is necessary that what is revealed come to pass, since otherwise what is false could form the basis of a prophecy.

[Reply.] I maintain that no revealed future contingent comes to pass necessarily; rather, contingently. I grant that 'this is revealed' was true at some time and that its [corresponding proposition] about the past was ever afterwards necessary. I grant also that it was not revealed as false, but as true and contingent (rather than as true and necessary). Consequently it could have been and can be false. Nevertheless the Prophets did not say what is false, since all prophecies regarding any future contingents were conditionals. But the condition was not always expressed. Sometimes it was expressed—as in the case of David and his throne[31]—and sometimes it was understood—as in the case of [the prophecy of] the destruction of Nineveh by the prophet Jonah: "Yet forty days, and Nineveh shall be overthrown"[32]—i.e., unless they would repent; and since they did repent, it was not destroyed.

[30]Cf. Ockham's *Quodlibeta*, IV, 4 (Boehner).
[31]Psalm 131 [132], 12 (Boehner): "If thy children will keep my covenant, and these my testimonies which I shall teach them: Their children also for evermore shall sit upon thy throne."
[32]Jonah 3, 4 (Boehner).

[ASSUMPTIONS]

K   In order to resolve these objections I first make certain assumptions. Once these are seen, the resolution of the arguments will be clear.

Assumption 1.[33] Neither active predestination nor active reprobation is a real thing distinct in some way or other from God or the divine Persons. Nor is passive predestination something absolute or relative distinct in some way from the person who is predestinate.[34] But the noun 'predestination' (or the concept), whether taken in the active or in the passive sense, signifies not only God Himself who will give eternal life to someone but also the person to whom it is given. Thus it signifies three things: God [who will give eternal life to someone], eternal life, and the person to whom it is given. Similarly, 'reprobation' signifies God who will give eternal punishment to someone, [eternal punishment, and the person to whom it is given].[35]

L   Assumption 2.[36] All propositions having to do with predestination and reprobation are contingent whether they are of present tense — e.g., 'God predestinates Peter' and 'Peter is predestinate' — or of past tense, or of future tense. If any [such proposition] were necessary, it would be one about the past. But 'Peter was predestinate,' for example, is neither a necessary proposition nor a proposition *de necessario*.[37] For I ask whether or not Peter could be

---

[33]Cf. Book One of Ockham's *Commentary on the Sentences* (the *Ordinatio*), d. 41, q. 1, **F** (Boehner).

[34]The first two sentences of Assumption 1 constitute Ockham's first explicit assertion of the position he took in response to Question I and which formed the ultimate basis of his replies to all the preceding objections.

[35]See note 22.

[36]At this point in the text Boehner has a note referring to Book One of Ockham's *Commentary on the Sentences* (the *Ordinatio*), d. 38, q. 1, **N**. (See Appendix I, pp. 90–91 below.) The passage referred to, however, does not bear directly on Assumption 2 but rather on Assumption 6.

[37]Ockham, *Expositio aurea* (Bologna, 1496), fol. 122c: "A necessary proposition

damned. If not, then necessarily he will be saved, and in that case there would be no need to deliberate or to take trouble – which is absurd.[38] If he can be damned, suppose that he is so in fact. Then 'Peter is damned' is true. Therefore after this instant 'Peter was damned' will always be true. But according to you[39] 'Peter was predestinate' is necessary. Therefore 'Peter was predestinate' and 'Peter was reprobate' will be true at one and the same time; and contradictories follow from these [propositions], as is clear. (Scotus, too, maintains this conclusion.)[40]

M   Assumption 3. Some propositions are about the present as regards both their wording and their subject matter (*secundum vocem et secundum rem*). Where such [propositions] are concerned, it is universally true that every true proposition about the present has [corresponding to it] a necessary one about the past – e.g., 'Socrates is seated,' 'Socrates is walking,' 'Socrates is just,' and the like.

Other propositions are about the present as regards their wording only and are equivalently about the future, since their truth depends on the truth of propositions about the future.[41] Where such [propositions] are concerned, the rule that every true proposition about the present has [corresponding to it] a necessary

---

is one that cannot be false. But a proposition *de necessario* is one that takes on such a mode [e.g., one to which the modal operator 'it is necessary that' has been applied]. Thus a proposition *de necessario* is sometimes true and sometimes false, sometimes necessary and sometimes impossible." (Quoted in Baudry, *Lexique*, art. "*Propositio necessaria*.")

[38]Ockham is quoting a key phrase from Aristotle's *De interpretatione*, Ch. 9, 18b26 ff. (See Appendix II, p. 101 below.)

[39]Evidently a reference to the objector represented in Objection 2.

[40]Cf. Duns Scotus, *Reportata Parisiensia*, I, d. 40, q. u., n. 11 (ed. Vivès, t. 22, p. 477), against St. Thomas Aquinas, *Summa theologica*, I, q. 14, a. 13. Cf. also Duns Scotus, *Opus Oxoniense*, I, d. 39, q. u., nn. 31–33 (ed. Vivès, t. 10, pp. 653 ff.). (Boehner) The conclusion that Scotus, too, maintains is the thesis of Assumption 2 – viz., that all propositions having to do with predestination and reprobation are contingent. Scotus's reasons for maintaining this are, however, somewhat different from Ockham's. According to Scotus 'predestination' properly signifies an act of the divine will, in particular the ordination by God of some rational creature to election, or to grace and glory. Every such act of the divine will is contingent rather than necessary. A past-tense proposition about such an act – e.g., 'God predestinated Peter' – does not come under the necessity of the past (is not necessary *per accidens*) because the act of the divine will to which it refers is not in the past but is rather always present in "the now of eternity." (See note 54 for other approaches to these problems along this line.)

[41]See note 16.

one about the past is not true. And this is not remarkable, since there are true propositions about the past and about the future that have no true [proposition] about the present [corresponding to them]. For example, 'what is white was black' and 'what is white will be black' are true while their [corresponding proposition] about the present — 'what is white is black' — is false.[42]

N   Assumption 4. All propositions having to do with predestination and reprobation, whether they are verbally about the present or about the past, are nevertheless equivalently about the future, since their truth depends on the truth of propositions formally about the future.[43] But Assumption 3 shows that such true [propositions] about the present do not have a necessary one about the past [corresponding to them] but rather one that is merely contingent, just as the one about the present is contingent. From these [considerations] it follows that no proposition about the present having to do with predestination and reprobation has a necessary one about the past [corresponding to it].

O   Assumption 5. From the Philosopher's point of view[44] God does not know one part of a contradiction [to be true] any more than [He knows] the other, not only as regards future contingents but also as regards those [propositions] about the present and about the past that are equivalent to propositions about the fu-

---

[42]Ockham's white/black example (see Appendix II, p. 100 below) and the observations with which he introduces it constitute a special case that cannot help to show that there is nothing remarkable in his claim that such a proposition as 'Peter is predestinate' — apparently about the present but really about the future — has no corresponding proposition about the past that is necessary *per accidens*. Ockham's point is that the present-tense proposition 'Peter is predestinate' is to be treated as a proposition whose truth has yet to be settled by what will be posited in actuality in the future (such as 'Socrates will be seated') and *not* as one whose truth is settled by what is posited in actuality in the present (such as 'Socrates is seated').

[43]A proposition "formally about the future" is a proposition about genuinely future things, about things that have yet to be settled — i.e., a future contingent proposition. Not every proposition "verbally about the future" is also formally about the future. See pp. 61–62. Assumption 4 is an explicit application of Assumption 3 to the present subject matter.

[44]Aristotle, *De interpretatione*, Ch. 9; cf. Ockham, *Expositio aurea*, on the conclusion of Book One of *De interpretatione; Summa logicae*, III (3), c. 31 (edn. Venet., 1508, fol. 89va–90ra and elsewhere); Book One of his *Commentary on the Sentences* (the *Ordinatio*), d. 38, q. v. M (Boehner) See Appendix I, pp. 89–90 below; Appendix II, pp. 105–107 below; Appendix III, pp. 110–113 below. See also Introduction, p. 12 above.

ture.[45] On the contrary, according to him neither [part of the con-tradiction] is known by God, since according to him in Book One of the *Posterior Analytics* [Ch. 2, 71b26] nothing is known unless it is true. But as regards these [propositions] truth is not determinate, since according to him no reason can be given why one part is true rather than the other. Consequently both parts will be true or nei-ther will be true. But it is not possible that both parts be true. Therefore neither is true. Therefore neither is known.

P   Assumption 6. It must be held beyond question that God knows with certainty all future contingents—i.e., He knows with certainty which part of the contradiction is[46] true and which false. (Nevertheless all such propositions as 'God knows that this part— or that part—of the contradiction is true' are contingent, not neces-sary, as has been said before.[47])

It is difficult, however, to see how He knows this [with certain-ty], since one part [of the contradiction] is no more determined to truth than the other. The Subtle Doctor[48] maintains that the divine intellect, insofar as it is in some respect prior[49] to the determination

---

[45]See note 16. Aristotle does not discuss God's knowledge in *De interpretatione*, Ch. 9, or in *Posterior Analytics*, Bk. I, Ch. 2. All that Ockham means to claim is that some of what Aristotle says in those passages applies to God's knowledge (in virtue of applying to all knowledge whatever).

[46]Reading '*est*' for '*erit*.' Suppose that the contradiction in question is that be-tween the future contingents 'Peter will be saved' and 'Peter will not be saved.' One or the other of these is true *now* and hence is known by God to be true now. This reading is confirmed by the wording of the example in the next sentence: "*Deus scit hanc partem contradictionis esse* [rather than *fore*] *veram vel illam.*"

[47]Evidently a reference to the end of Ockham's reply to Objection 5 (p. 42).

[48]Duns Scotus, *Opus Oxoniense*, I, d. 39, q. u., n. 23 (ed. Vivès, t. 10, p. 639); *Re-portatio*, I, d. 38, q. 2, nn. 3-4 (t. 22, pp. 469 ff.). Cf. Book One of Ockham's *Commen-tary on the Sentences* (the *Ordinatio*), d. 38, q. 1, **D**. [Appendix I, pp. 83-84 below.] (Boehner)

[49]Scotus maintains that the divine intellect is *naturally* (although not temporally prior to the determination of the divine will. This is a special case under his general principle that an act of understanding is naturally (although not always temporally) prior to an act of will. (See, e.g., *Reportata Parisiensia*, I.1, d. 17, q. 3, n. 3 [ed. Vivès, t. 22, p. 213]; *Opus Oxoniense*, I.1, d. 17, q. 4, n. 5 [ed. Vivès, t. 10, p. 104]; I.3, d. 18, n. 20 [ed. Vivès, t. 14, p. 703]. See especially *Opus Oxoniense*, I, d. 2, q. 1, art, ii ["Absolute Properties of God"], part i ["Intellect and Will"], in Allan B. Wolter, *Duns Scotus: Philosophical Writings* [Latin and English], Edinburgh and New York, Nelson, 1962, pp. 52-61.) When Scotus says that God at one instant apprehends those com-plexes and at another, subsequent instant determines that one part is true and at another, subsequent instant knows that part to be true, he is speaking not of instants of time but of "instants of nature." To say that *A* is naturally but not temporally prior to *B* is to say that *B* occurs at an instant of nature subsequent to that at which *A*

of the divine will, apprehends those complexes[50] as neutral with respect to itself, and then* the divine will determines that one part [of the contradiction] is true for some instant, willing that the other part is false[51] for that same instant. After the determination of the divine will is effected, however, the divine intellect sees the determination of its own will, which is immutable. It sees clearly that one part is true with certainty — viz., that part which its own will wills to be true.

I argue* against this opinion, however, for [in the first place] it does not seem to preserve the certainty of God's knowledge in respect of future things that depend absolutely on a created will.[52] For I ask whether or not the determination of a created will necessarily follows the determination of the divine will. If it does, then the will necessarily acts [as it does], just as fire does, and so merit and demerit are done away with. If it does not, then the determination of a created will is required for knowing determinately one or the other part of a contradiction regarding those [future things that depend absolutely on a created will]. For the determination of the uncreated will does not suffice, because a created will can oppose the determination [of the uncreated will]. Therefore, since the determination of the [created] will was not from eternity, God did not have certain cognition of the things that remained [for a created will to determine].

Secondly, when something is determined contingently, so that it is still possible that it is not determined and it is possible that it was never determined, then one cannot have certain and infallible cognition based on such a determination. But the determination of the divine will in respect of future contingents is such a determination, both according to him [Scotus] and in truth. Therefore God cannot have certain cognition of future contingents based on such a determination.

---

occurs although *A* and *B* occur at one and the same instant of time, or although *A* and *B* cannot be located in time at all. Ockham rejects Scotus's doctrine of "instants of nature." See Question III, pp. 71–72 (especially n. 104) and Appendix I, pp. 81–83 (especially n. 7).

[50]See note 24.

[51]Reading '*falsam*' for '*veram*.'

[52]See Question I, Oobjection 3, pp. 39–40. See also Introduction, pp. 17–20 above, on the antecedent and the consequent disposing will of God.

[The argument] is supported as follows. All such propositions as 'God from eternity willed this part of the contradiction* to be true' and 'God from eternity determined this' are contingent, as is clear from Assumption 2. Consequently they can be true and [they can be] false. Therefore one will have no certain cognition based on such a determination.

For that reason I maintain[53] that it is impossible to express clearly the way in which God knows future contingents. Nevertheless it must be held that He does so, but contingently. That must be held because of the pronouncements of the Saints, who say that God does not know things that are becoming in a way different from that in which [He knows] things that have already occurred.[54]

Despite [the impossibility of expressing it clearly], the following way [of knowing future contingents] can be ascribed [to God]. Just as the [human] intellect on the basis of one and the same [intuitive] cognition of certain non-complexes can have evident cognition of contradictory contingent propositions such as 'A exists,' 'A does not exist,' in the same way it can be granted that the divine essence is intuitive cognition that is so perfect, so clear, that it is evident cognition of all things past and future, so that it knows which part of a contradiction [involving such things] is* true and which part false.[55]

[53]Cf. Book One of Ockham's *Commentary on the Sentences* (the *Ordinatio*), d. 38, q. u., M [Appendix I, pp. 89–90 below]. (Boehner)

[54]What "must be held because of the pronouncements of the Saints" is evidently only that God does know future contingents *determinately*—this much is confirmed by what Ockham reports of them—and not also that His knowledge of them is contingent. Both St. Thomas Aquinas (in *Summa theologica*, I, q. 14, a. 13 [see Boehner, "Ockham's *Tractatus* . . . ," p. 435]) and St. Anselm (in *On the Harmony of the Foreknowledge, the Predestination, and the Grace of God with Free Choice*), for example, maintain that God knows all things, past, present, and future, as eternally present to Himself. The same sort of account of God's knowledge of temporal things can be found much earlier in Boethius as well (in *The Consolation of Philosophy*, V). Ockham's position is plainly opposed to that of St. Thomas (*loc. cit.*), who held that God's knowledge is necessary even though the things known by Him are contingent.

[55]Ockham's suggested account of the nature of God's knowledge of future contingents is somewhat obscured by the occurrence in this sentence of (*a*) inaccuracies of expression and (*b*) technical terms deriving from his theory of knowledge. As to (*a*), what he seems to have intended in the first part of the analogy might better have been expressed as follows: "Just as the human intellect on the basis of one and the same intuitive cognition of a non-complex such as *A* can have evident cognition of the present existence or nonexistence of *A* so that it knows which one of the contra-

Suppose it is said that that which is not true in itself cannot be known by anyone, but that [the proposition] that I shall sit down tomorrow is of that sort.

In that case I maintain that [that proposition] is true, so that [it *is*] not false, but *contingently* true, since it *can* be false.

On the contrary: each part of this [contradiction] 'I shall sit down tomorrow,' 'I shall not sit down tomorrow,' can, indifferently, be true. Therefore one part is not more true than the other.[56] Hence either neither is now true or both [are now true]. Not both; therefore neither.

I maintain that one part is now determinately true, so that [it is] not false, since God wills the one part to be true and the other to be false. Nevertheless He wills contingently. Therefore He can *not* will the one part and He can will the other part, inasmuch as the other part can come to pass.[57]

Q   Assumption 7.[58] In connection with the subject of predestination and reprobation the verb 'to know' (*scire*) is taken either broadly—i.e., for the cognition of anything whatever—and in that sense God knows (*cognoscit*) all things, non-complexes as well as complexes, necessary, contingent, false, and impossible; or strictly, and in that sense it is the same as to know (*cognoscere*) what is true.

---

dictory present contingent propositions '*A* exists,' '*A* does not exist' is true, in the same way it can be granted that . . ." As to (*b*), the terms 'evident cognition' and 'intuitive cognition' can be understood thoroughly only within Ockham's epistemology, which is most readily accessible in the translated material in Part II of Boehner's *Ockham: Philosophical Writings* ([Latin and English] Edinburgh and New York. Nelson, 1957: [English only] New York, Library of Liberal Arts, 1964). (Cf. also Baudry, *Lexique*, art. "*Notitia*.") It is enough for present purposes to say that evident cognition is indubitable cognition and that "intuitive cognition of a thing is that cognition in virtue of which it can be known whether or not the thing exists, so that if the thing does exist the intellect judges immediately that it exists and has evident cognition that it exists . . ." (in Book One of Ockham's *Commentary on the Sentences* (the *Ordinatio*), Prologus, q. 1, **Z**). The gist of Ockham's suggestion thus seems to be that all things past and future are objects of intuitive cognition for God in the way in which a presently existent thing can be an object of intuitive cognition for a human being.

[56]This objection is obviously intended as an allusion to the position attributed to Aristotle in Assumption 5.

[57]For a discussion of Ockham's remarks here, see Introduction, pp. 20–26 above.

[58]Cf. Book One of Ockham's *Commentary on the Sentences* (the *Ordinatio*), d. 39, q. 1, **B** (Appendix I, pp. 92–93 below), where Ockham distinguishes the same two senses of 'to know' as are distinguished in Assumption 7.

It is in this sense that the Philosopher says in Book One of the *Posterior Analytics* [Ch. 2, 71b26] that nothing is known unless it is true.

R   Assumption 8.[59] Some propositions having to do with predestination and reprobation are to be distinguished with respect to composition and division, such as those in which a mode is posited together with a clause in indirect discourse (*ponitur modus cum dicto*).[60] The result is that what is indicated (*denotatur*) in the sense of composition is that the mode is predicated of the prejacent of the clause in indirect discourse, or of the proposition belonging to that clause.[61] What is indicated in the sense of division, however, is that the predicate belonging to the clause in indirect discourse, or to the proposition belonging to that clause, is predicated together with such a mode of that for which the subject of the clause supposits, as is shown in logic.[62] This shows that 'the predestinate

[59]Cf. Book One of Ockham's *Commentary on the Sentences* (the *Ordinatio*), d. 40, q. 1, C. Cf. also Duns Scotus, *Opus Oxoniense*, I, d. 39, q. u., n. 17 (ed. Vivès, t. 10, pp. 629 ff.) and d. 40, q.u., n. 2 (pp. 680 ff.). With respect to the logic, cf. Ockham's *Summa logicae*, II, c. 9. (Boehner)

[60]In *Summa logicae*, II, c. 9, Ockham distinguishes between modal propositions that do not contain a clause in indirect discourse (a "*dictum*") and those that do contain one. The latter are called "*de modo*" propositions. A *de modo* proposition, he says, "is always to be distinguished with respect to composition and division. In the sense of composition what is indicated is always that the mode is verified of [see note 28] the proposition belonging to the *dictum*. Thus what is indicated by 'that every man is an animal is necessary' [in the sense of composition] is that the mode 'necessary' will be verified of the proposition 'every man is an animal,' the *dictum* of which is that which is said (*dicitur*) — viz., 'that every man is an animal.' For it is called a *dictum* of a proposition when the terms are taken in the accusative case and the verb in the infinitive mood [the regular Latin construction for indirect discourse]. But the sense of division of such a [*de modo*] proposition is always equipollent to the proposition taken together with the mode and without the *dictum*. Thus 'that every man is an animal is necessary' in the sense of division is equipollent to 'every man of necessity (or necessarily) is an animal'" (ed. Boehner, p. 246). In *Summa logicae*, II, c. 10, Ockham says that modal propositions of the other sort, those that do not contain a *dictum*, are "entirely equipollent to propositions with a *dictum* [*de modo* propositions] understood in the sense of division." He then observes that a *de modo* proposition may be true in the sense of composition and false in the sense of division, or vice versa, introducing the following as one of his examples: ". . . this is true — 'that everything true is true is necessary' — and nevertheless this is false — 'everything true necessarily is true'" (pp. 248–249).

[61]The "prejacent" of, or the proposition "belonging to" the *dictum* 'that every man is an animal' is 'every man is an animal.' This difference is more apparent grammatically in Latin, where the corresponding *dictum* is '*omnem hominem esse animal*' and its prejacent is '*omnis homo est animal.*'

[62]The notion of a term's suppositing something is part of the theory of the properties of terms developed by thirteenth-century logicians (see, e.g., Kretzmann,

can be damned' and [propositions] like it are not to be distinguished with respect to composition and division.[63]

S   Assumption 9.[64] For present purposes 'cause' is taken in two ways. In one way for a real thing having another real thing as its effect. That from whose existence something else follows is called the cause, for when it is posited the effect is posited, and when it is not posited [the effect] cannot be posited.

It is used in another way when it means (*importat*) the priority of one proposition over another with respect to an inference. We say, for instance, that when there is a natural inference from one proposition to another and not vice versa, the antecedent is the cause of the consequent and not vice versa.[65]

Once these [assumptions] have been seen one can respond to the arguments that have been propounded, proving that the predestinate can be damned, and also to other [arguments] propounded for other questions concerning God's knowledge in respect of future contingents.

William of Sherwood's Introduction to Logic, especially Chapter Five) and discussed extensively by Ockham (in *Summa logicae,* I, c. 63—c. 77, some of which appears in English in Part IV of Boehner's *Ockham: Philosophical Writings*). For present purposes it is enough to say that "that for which the subject of the clause supposits" is what is named or referred to by means of the subject-term in the *dictum* of a *de modo* proposition. Applying this remark of Ockham's to the proposition 'that Socrates is an animal is necessary' we may say that if the proposition is understood in the sense of division, then what is understood is that animality is predicated with necessity of the man Socrates, as in 'Socrates necessarily is an animal.'

[63]The 'not' in this sentence appears in most manuscripts of the *Treatise* but is omitted from one and erased in another. Everything else in Assumption 8 (as well as the discussion in *Summa logicae,* II, c. 9 and c. 10) suggests that the 'not' does belong here. 'The predestinate can be damned' is a modal proposition but not a *de modo* proposition. It should, then, be equipollent to the corresponding *de modo* proposition understood in the sense of division (see note 60). The corresponding *de modo* proposition is 'that the predestinate is damned is possible.' In the sense of composition this is understood as "'the predestinate is damned' is possible," which Ockham denies. In the sense of division it is understood as 'the predestinate possibly is damned,' which Ockham maintains is true, and to which 'the predestinate can be damned' is equipollent.

[64]Cf. Book One of Ockham's *Commentary on the Sentences* (the *Ordinatio*), d. 41, q. 1, F (Boehner).

[65]On an antecedent as cause of a consequent or a premiss as cause of a conclusion cf. Aristotle, especially *Posterior Analytics,* Book II, Ch. 11 (94a20); also *Metaphysics,* Book V, Ch. 2 (1013b17).

[QUESTION II]

A   In respect of all future contingents does God have determinate, certain, infallible, immutable, necessary cognition of one part of a contradiction?[66]

[Article I]

[The following arguments are advanced to show] that it is not determinate.

(1) Neither truth nor falsity is determinate in future contingents. Therefore [God does not have determinate cognition of one part of a contradiction between future contingents].

(2) If it were determinate, then whether or not we deliberated [about something] necessarily that which is known by God determinately would come to pass. Consequently we would deliberate and take trouble in vain.[67]

(3) If it were determinate, then God would be of limited knowledge.* Proof: If God can bring about something determinately, so that He cannot [bring about] its opposite, He is of determinate and limited power. Therefore, similarly, [if God could know one part of a contradiction between future contingents determinately so that He could not know its opposite, He would be of determinate and limited knowledge].[68]

---

[66]Ockham follows Duns Scotus's divisions in the following Articles. Cf. Scotus's *Opus Oxoniense*, I, d. 39, q. u., n. 1 (ed. Vivès, t. 10, p. 613); *Reportata Parisiensia*, I, dd. 38 and 39, qq. 1 and 2 (t. 22, pp. 468 ff.). Cf. also Alexander of Hales, *Summa theologica*, I, nn. 184-187 (edn. Quaracchi, t. 1, pp. 269-275). (Boehner)

[67]See note 38. See also Introduction, pp. 12-16, above, on the derivation of arguments (1), (2), and (4).

[68]We have supplied this conclusion in order to bring out plainly the analogical character of the argument. That it is an argument from analogy is shown by the occurrence of the word 'similarly' just before the conclusion is left to be supplied

54

(4) Whatever is not determinately* true in itself is not known by God with determinate cognition. But a future contingent is of that sort. Therefore [God does not have determinate cognition of one part of a contradiction between future contingents].

The Faith is in opposition [to all these arguments].

B   In reply to this part of the question I maintain* that, as was said in Assumption 6, God has determinate cognition in respect of future contingents since He knows determinately which part of the contradiction will be true and which false.

Reply to (1). It is clear from Assumption 5 what must be said, for from the Philosopher's point of view neither part [of the contradiction] is determinately true in the case of future contingents that depend absolutely on a free power—e.g., on a created will. This is clear in the same [Assumption]. What must be said in accordance with truth and the Faith, however, is clear from Assumption 6.

Reply to (2). The first consequence does not hold good, for although He does know one part [of the contradiction] determinately, nevertheless He knows contingently, and He can *not* know, and He can[69] never have known. Therefore, deliberation does make a difference.

Reply to (3). I deny the [first] consequence. As to the proof, I grant that it is true that if God were to cause one part of a contradiction in such a way that He could not cause the other, then He would be of limited power. Similarly, if He were to know one part [of the contradiction] in such a way that He could not know the other, then He would have limited and imperfect knowledge. But neither [of these antecedents] is true.

Reply to (4). It is clear that the minor premiss is false. Nevertheless, [although a future contingent is determinately true,] it is true contingently, for it can be false and it could never have been true.

(*igitur similiter, etc.*) and by the character of Ockham's reply to it (on p. 55). In order to read it as an argument from analogy, however, we have had to adopt a rare variant in the first sentence. Of the eight manuscripts and one fifteenth-century printed text on which Boehner's edition is based only one manuscript has '*scientiae*' ('knowledge'). The other eight sources all have '*potentiae*' ('power'), which obliterates the point of the argument.

[69]Reading '*potest*' for '*potuit.*'

[Article II][70]

C   In the second part of the question it is principally argued*
that He does not have certain and infallible cognition.

(1) Proof: 'God cognized (*novit*) that I would sit down tomorrow, and I shall not sit down tomorrow; therefore He is deceived.'
This inference is clear, for in believing that that is in fact the case
which is not in fact the case He is deceived. Similarly, then: 'God
cognized that I would sit down tomorrow, and it is possible that
I shall not sit down tomorrow; therefore it is possible that He be
deceived,* and consequently He can be deceived.' This second inference is proved as follows: just as an assertoric conclusion
follows from two assertoric premises,* so a *de possibili* conclusion
follows from [two premises] one of which is assertoric and the
other *de possibili*.[71]

(2) If God cognized that I would sit down tomorrow, and it is
possible that* I shall not sit down tomorrow, suppose that in fact I
shall not sit down tomorrow. Then it follows that God is deceived.
Since what is impossible does not follow from the positing in fact of
what is possible, 'God is deceived' is not impossible.

The Faith is in opposition [to both these arguments].

D   I maintain that He does have certain and infallible cognition. This is proved by means of Assumption 6.

Reply to (1) in opposition. I maintain that the first inference is
good, although not syllogistic. For to be deceived is to think that a
thing is otherwise than it is for the time for which it is believed to be
so. And this is what is entailed by those assertoric premises, for
they entail that God believes otherwise than will be the case. And
the conclusion follows from those two premises if they can be true
at one and the same time. But they cannot be true at one and the

---

[70]Cf. Duns Scotus, *Opus Oxoniense*, I, d. 39, q. u., nn. 1 and 3 (ed. Vivès, t. 10, p.
613), where these arguments are to be found nearly word for word. Scotus's solu-
tions to them appear in n. 27 (t. 10, p. 651). (Boehner)

[71]On assertoric propositions see note 7. A *de possibili* proposition is a *de modo*
proposition (see note 60) involving the mode 'possible.' The rule of inference ap-
pealed to may be expressed as follows: If '*p* and *q*, therefore *r*' is the form of an acceptable inference, then '*p* and it is possible that *q*, therefore it is possible that *r*' is the
form of an acceptable inference.

same time, for if God cognized that I would sit down tomorrow it follows that 'I shall sit down tomorrow' is true, for nothing is known unless it is true. Therefore its opposite is false, since otherwise contradictories would be true at one and the same time.

But whatever is the case regarding the first inference, it is certain that* the second does not hold good. In order for such a mixed inference (*mixtio*) to hold good the major premiss would have to be omnitemporally assertoric (*de inesse simpliciter*), so that it would always be necessarily true, however much that *de possibili* premiss should be posited in fact. In that case the *de possibili* conclusion follows; otherwise not.[72] I prove this claim in the following way. If we argue from the opposite of the conclusion together with that same *de possibili* premiss we infer only the opposite of a necessary omnitemporally assertoric proposition. In truth, then,* from 'God cannot be deceived' and 'it is possible that I shall not sit down tomorrow' only this conclusion follows: 'God knows (*scit*) not necessarily but only contingently that I shall sit down tomorrow.' There-

---

[72]Ockham's treatment of the second inference in argument (1) is not easy to follow. It is not hard to see that he is right to reject the inference; the difficulties arise in considering his stated reasons for doing so. For one thing, he uses technical terms that are used elsewhere in the *Treatise* (see p. 70) but are not defined in the *Treatise* A "mixed inference" is an inference involving either assertoric and modal propositions (as here) or modal propositions governed by different modes. (Ockham discusses many varieties of both sorts of mixed inference in *Summa logicae*, III (1), c. 31-c. 64; ed. Boehner, pp. 402–456.) An "omnitemporally assertoric" proposition is an assertoric proposition "in which the predicate cannot be attached to the subject at one time and denied of it at another time, but [the proposition] is constituted uniformly at all times, so that [the predicate] is predicated truly either always or never" (*Summa logicae*, III (1), c. 31; p. 403). It is distinguished in Ockham's logic from a "temporally assertoric" (*de inesse ut nunc*) proposition, "in which the predicate can be truly affirmed of the subject at one time and truly denied at another time" (*loc. cit.*). Given this distinction (which Ockham evidently considers exhaustive), it looks as if he is here claiming that the objector's major premiss — 'God cognized that I would sit down tomorrow' — is not a necessary omnitemporally assertoric proposition, and that the inference is therefore invalid. Ockham's reply would have been justified if the objector had used the word 'knew' (*scivit*) rather than 'cognized' (*novit*); for 'God knew that I would sit down tomorrow' is, from Ockham's point of view, a future contingent proposition despite its being verbally about the past. The premiss as the objector has it, however, is not a future contingent proposition but a proposition necessary about the past and hence one that satisfies Ockham's demand. Ockham may have misconstrued these arguments by interpreting 'cognized' as if it were 'knew.' (See his truth-value-neutral use of '*notitia*' in Assumption 6.) Notice that in his reply to (1) Ockham twice uses a form of '*scio*' rather than of '*nosco*.'

fore in order for the first mixed inference to hold good the major premiss would have to be omnitemporally assertoric. But* it is clear that it is not so, for it is merely contingent, inasmuch as it can be true and can be false and can never have been true. This is clear from Assumptions 2 and 3 above.

Reply to (2). I maintain that what is impossible never follows solely from the positing in fact of a *de possibili** proposition. Nevertheless the assertoric proposition ['I shall not sit down tomorrow'] in which the *de possibili* proposition is posited can be inconsistent with an assertoric proposition with which the posited *de possibili* proposition is not inconsistent. (For an antecedent can be inconsistent with something with which its consequent is not inconsistent, as whiteness is inconsistent with something with which color is not inconsistent.) And that assertoric proposition entails the *de possibili* proposition, and not vice versa, as is clear. Therefore from that assertoric proposition, which is an antecedent for the *de possibili* proposition, and another assertoric proposition inconsistent with the first there can follow an impossible conclusion that* does not follow from that *de possibili* proposition, which is a consequent, and the other assertoric proposition. So it is no wonder that an impossible conclusion follows from incompossible premisses, for an impossible conclusion does follow from opposite premisses in a syllogism.

In reply to what is claimed [in (2)] I now maintain that nothing impossible follows from 'it is possible that I shall not sit down tomorrow' when it is posited in fact. But from 'I shall not sit down tomorrow,' in which it is posited in fact, and 'God cognized that I would sit down tomorrow' the impossible proposition 'God is mistaken' does follow; and it does so because the premisses are incompossible. For example, 'Socrates is seated' and 'Socrates can stand' are true at one and the same time. Nevertheless 'Socrates is seated' and 'Socrates is standing' do not hold good at one and the same time but rather are inconsistent; therefore it follows from those two propositions that sitting is standing. That conclusion does not follow, however, from 'Socrates is seated' and 'Socrates can stand.' The whole cause [of the difficulty] is the inconsistency of the premisses in the uniform [inference] and the lack of it in the mixed inference. And in the same way in all respects this is [the whole cause of the difficulty] in what is claimed [in (2)].

[Article III][73]

E   Third, it is argued that He does not have immutable knowledge (*scientiam*)[74] regarding future contingents.

[Part One]

(1) There can be no passage from contradictory to contradictory without any change.[75] Proof: It does not seem that that which was true earlier is now false, or vice versa, unless there is some change. But God knowing the contingent proposition 'I shall sit down'[76] can *not* know it, for it can be false, and what is false is not known.[77]

(2) Similarly: God does not now know the proposition 'I am in Rome,' for this is now false, and He can now know it for the year when it will be true. Therefore it seems that God changes.[78]

---

[73]Cf. Duns Scotus, *Opus Oxoniense*, I, d. 39, q. u., nn. 1, 3, and 4 (ed. Vivès, t. 10, pp. 613–614); also Book One of Ockham's *Commentary on the Sentences* (the *Ordinatio*), d. 39, q. u. [Appendix 1, pp. 92–95 below]. (Boehner)

[74]Although Ockham used '*notitia*' ('cognition') in framing Question II originally and in the specific questions of Articles I and II, he uses '*scientia*' ('knowledge') in the specific questions of Articles III and IV.

[75]I.e., He cannot first know the one part of a contradiction and then know the other part without changing.

[76]All the examples using direct discourse and the pronoun 'I' in this argument and the two following should have used either indirect discourse or a proper name in place of the pronoun, since the 'I' of the examples is surely not intended to refer to God but rather to the framer of the arguments.

[77]The point of argument (1) is brought out more easily by using the example supplied by Ockham in what is evidently his reply to it (on p. 61). Consider only all times prior to t_1, and suppose that the proposition 'Socrates will sit down at t_1' is true and therefore known by God. Since the proposition is contingent, it can be false and hence God's knowledge can be otherwise than it is. But this is not to say that God's knowledge admits of change; in particular, it is not to say that God's knowledge passes over from the one contradictory to the other, which is the sufficient condition laid down by the objector himself at the outset of the argument. In his reply, therefore, Ockham bases his criticism on the assumption that the objector meant to show that it is possible that God *first know* and *afterwards not know* before t_1 that Socrates will sit down at t_1.

[78]The second premiss of argument (2) — "He can now know it for the year when it will be true" (*potest eam scire modo ad annum, quando erit vera*) — is obscure. It seems to suggest that although God does not now know 'Peter is in Rome,' He can now know 'Peter is in Rome at t_n' (assuming that Peter is not now in Rome but will be there at t_n). But that observation could scarcely be construed as supporting the conclusion, nor is it the sort of point to which Ockham's reply is addressed. In view of these discrepancies it seems that the second premiss was to have been "He will know it in the year when it will be true"—i.e., at t_n God will know 'Peter is in Rome.' This reading

(3) Similarly: He now knows this proposition about the future —'I shall read tomorrow' (suppose that this is true)—and after tomorrow He will not know the proposition 'I shall read[79] tomorrow,' for then it will be false.

F   [Reply to (2).] Speaking of propositions that are merely about the present and that depend in no way on the future, I maintain that just as such propositions can change from truth to falsity and vice versa, so God can at one time know such a proposition* and at another time not, and know one* after He did not know it, and not know after He did know, and know a proposition that He did not know earlier, without any change in Him as a result of a mere change in a creature or in known propositions of this sort (just as He is said to be first noncreating and afterwards creating as a result of a change in and the establishing of a creature), because *our* intellect can [do this] without any change in it. Proof: Suppose that I think that the proposition 'Socrates is seated' is true although it is false, because Socrates is standing, and that while that act remains in my intellect that proposition becomes true. Now I know that which I did not know before, without any change in my intellect but only in the thing.[80] And it is in this way that that passage "in relation there is no motion" in Book VII of the *Physics* is understood, so that the proposition is particular rather than universal. For the Philosopher intends there to speak of knowledge, since it is a relation, [and to say of it] that someone can begin to know something without any change in him, as has been said.[81] Moreover, as

---

may reasonably be considered to support the stated conclusion, and it seems to provide the sort of point to which Ockham's reply is addressed. There is, however, no feasible reading of argument (2) that connects it specifically with the question of the immutability of God's knowledge regarding *future* contingents, the topic of this Article III. The opening words of Ockham's reply show that he was aware of this.

[79]Reading *'legam'* for *'legem.'*

[80]Ockham's reply to argument (2) seems to go wrong in two respects. In the first place, it is difficult if not impossible to accept his example as providing an instance of my first not knowing and then *knowing* that Socrates is seated while my belief remains unchanged. That what I believe to be the case is in fact the case is a necessary but not a sufficient condition for my knowing it to be the case. Secondly, and more important, even if Ockham's example did provide the instance he intended it to provide for *our* intellect, such an instance could not be provided for God's intellect. Since God is omniscient, it is impossible that God believes before t_n that Peter is in Rome and hence impossible that God first (before t_n) does not know and afterwards (at t_n) does know that Peter is in Rome while his belief remains unchanged.

[81]The passage Ockham quotes seems to be from Chapter 3 of Book VII of the *Physics* (246b11): ". . . relations are neither themselves qualitative modifications nor

the Commentator says, that proposition is stated in accord with Plato's view.[82]

[Reply to (1).] But speaking of propositions that are about the future, I draw the following distinction. Some future [contingents] do not convey (*important*) anything present or past. It is impossible that God first know and afterwards not know such future [contingents], for it is impossible that God [first] know and afterwards not know before t_1 'Socrates will sit down at t_1.' And the cause [of this impossibility] is that before t_1 it cannot first be true and afterwards false. Rather, if it is true before t_1 it was always true before t_1, for every proposition that is simply about the future was always true if it is ever true.

[Reply to (3).] Other [contingents] that are future as regards their wording suggest (*implicant*) that present or past things are

---

yet subjects of such modification or of coming-into-being or of any kind of change at all." But what Ockham goes on to say of Aristotle's view makes it plain that he is drawing far more directly on this later passage from the same chapter (247b1 ff.):

"Nor are the states of the intellectual part qualitative modifications, nor do they ever come into existence in the primary and strict sense. For it is even more true of the state of knowing that it is of the moral virtues that it is a condition determined by a particular relation; and it is further evident that these intellectual states have no proper genesis. For that which knows potentially comes to know actually not in virtue of any motion of its own, but because something not itself is now newly presented to it; when the particular is presented to it, it gets such knowledge as it can have of the particular by means of knowledge of the universal. And again the enjoyment and actualizing of knowledge is not the result of a process of coming-into-being, unless you choose to say the same of every act of seeing or touching and consider the actualizing of knowing as analogous to such. Nor is the original acquisition of knowledge a process of becoming or a modification. For it is when the understanding has come to rest at its goal that we are said to know and possess a truth, and there is no process of becoming leading to the terminal pause, nor indeed to any kind of change, as has already been shown. Again, just as we do not say that a man has come to have knowledge again when he emerges from drunkenness or sleep or disease (although it is true that his power of realizing knowledge has been suspended), so likewise we should not say that when he originally acquires the state, he is 'coming to be' possessed of knowledge."

At least two passages from Aristotle's *Categories*, as well, seem highly relevant to Ockham's reply to argument (2) — viz., Ch. 5, 4a22 ff.; Ch. 7, 7b23 ff.

[82]We have not located this remark in Averroes ("the Commentator"). If "that proposition" is the general principle that a relation may begin to obtain between A and B without any change in A, it may be said to be "in accord with Plato's view" as expressed, for example, in *Theaetetus*, 155B–C. On the other hand, the more specific principle that "someone can begin to know something without any change in him" might be construed as an echo of the familiar Platonic account of beginning-to-

future. Suppose, for example, that the proposition 'Socrates will sit down at t_1' is asserted after t_1. This suggests that past things are future—viz., that t_1 is future and that the sitting down is future. Such a proposition about the future can change from truth to falsity, since before t_1 it was true and after t_1 it is false. And God can *not* know such a future contingent after He *did* know it, as a result of change in things and the passage of time, without any change on His part.

Regarding these latter future [contingents] it must be known that some of them are true and do not begin to be true but do begin to be false. If, for example, t_1 is tomorrow, 'Socrates will sit down at t_1' (suppose that is the case) is true now. It never began to be true, but it will begin to be false, for after t_1 it will always be false. And 'Socrates is predestinate' is of this kind, since before the [giving of] supreme blessedness it is always true if it is ever true, but after the [giving of] supreme blessedness it will always be false.

Others of them are false and never begin to be false but do begin to be true. For example, 'Socrates will not sit down at t_1,' since before t_1 it will always be false (suppose that is the case) and afterwards it will always be true. And 'Socrates is not predestinate' is of this kind, since before the [giving of] supreme blessedness it was false and afterwards it will always be true.

G   [*Part Two*]

The same point [viz., that God does not have immutable knowledge regarding future contingents] is argued for as follows. God can know more than He does know, for He can know many contingent propositions that will be true but that are now false. Similarly, He can know less than He does know, for He knows some propositions that are true about the present and that will be false ever afterwards. Therefore His knowledge is mutable.

Speaking of knowing and of God's knowledge *strictly*, as is said in Assumption 7, I maintain that God can know something that He does not know now (since in this sense [of 'know'] God knows nothing unless it is true), for a proposition that is not true now—

---

know in terms of recollecting what is already known (see, e.g., *Phaedo*, 75E); and, indeed, Aristotle's example of the recovery of knowledge after drunkenness, sleep, or disease (see note 81) provides a picture strongly reminiscent of Plato's doctrine of recollection.

such as that I am in Rome—can be known by God at some time even though it is not known by Him now. Still it need not be granted that He can know more than He does know, for nothing is known by God unless it is true and everything true is known by God. But there are always equally many truths, and so there are always equally many things known by God.

I prove the assumption in the following way. It is not possible that there are more truths at one time than at another, for it is always the case that one or the other part of a contradiction is [true], and nothing is true unless it is one or the other part of a contradiction. Nor is it possible that both parts of a contradiction be true. Hence there are as many truths at one time as at another, neither more nor less, even though something is true at one time that is not true at another. And [this holds good] universally, so that if something that was true before becomes false, something that was false before becomes true. Thus this does not follow: 'God can know many things that He does not know, and not know many things that He does know; therefore He can know more, or less, than He does know.'

Suppose someone says that whatever God knows now He will always know, since from the fact that God first knows the proposition 'Socrates is seated' and afterwards knows the proposition 'Socrates was seated' [it does] not [follow] that He knows something different; rather, [He knows] one and the same thing.[83]

I maintain that if one takes 'knowledge' or 'know' for that cognition of God's whereby He cognizes those propositions, then that [knowledge of His] is one and the same in respect of all things knowable. If, however, one takes God's knowing according as it involves the complexes 'Socrates is seated,' 'Socrates was seated,' then it is not one and the same. For those complexes are neither one and the same, nor equivalent,* nor interchangeable (*convertibilia*); for the one can be true while the other is false.[84] Suppose

---

[83]This paragraph suggests a view like the views advanced by Boethius, Anselm, and Aquinas (see note 54), who maintained that God knows *all* contingent things from the viewpoint of eternity as we know *present* contingent things. On this view God does not first know one proposition—'Socrates is seated at t_1'—and then know another—'Socrates was seated at t_1'; rather He knows from eternity the eternally present fact of Socrates's sitting at t_1.

[84]Ockham would have put his point more precisely if he had said "for it can be that the one is true while the other is false."

that God knows now for the first time the proposition 'Socrates is seated.' In that case the proposition "God knows the proposition 'Socrates was seated' " is false about the past. Similarly, when Socrates is walking He knows the proposition 'Socrates was seated,' since this is true, and not the proposition 'Socrates is seated,' since this is false.[85]

H   **[Part Three]**

[It is argued that] His knowledge can increase, for He can know more than He does know; and it can decrease, for He can know less than He does know. Therefore [God's knowledge] can change.

I maintain that it can neither increase nor decrease, for it is undifferentiated (*indistincta*) in respect of all things.[86] But can the number of foreknown things really be increased or decreased? It can be said that this is false in the sense of composition,[87] for 'the number of the predestinate is increased or decreased' is impossible, since that means that the number of the predestinate is first greater and afterwards becomes less, or vice versa. And this is false, for these opposites cannot be verified successively, since whoever is predestinate has been predestinate from eternity. For every proposition that is simply about the future, that does not connote anything past or present, has always been true if it is ever true.

In the sense of division it can be granted, for then no more is meant than that someone besides those who are now predestinate can be predestinate, and this is true. But if that proposition is pos-

---

[85]This reply of Ockham's may be better understood in the light of his suggestion as to how God knows future contingents (on pp. 50, 89–90). In this reply he distinguishes two senses of 'God's knowledge.' God's knowledge in the first sense is that "intuitive cognition" which "is the divine essence," that single act of apprehension which is eternally one and the same and in which everything knowable is known in a single eternal intuitive cognition. In this first sense 'God's knowledge' refers only to His act of cognition and not to the relation of that act to the world. In the second sense assigned by Ockham to 'God's knowledge' it refers not just to God's act of cognition but also to the relation of that act of cognition to the world.

[86]Ockham's point here seems to be that when God's knowledge is understood to be His single essential eternal intuitive cognition (see note 85), the object of God's knowledge is the single undifferentiated eternal object that includes all things—whether complex or simple; necessary, possible, or impossible; true or false. Cf. Appendix I, p. 93.

[87]See Assumption 8 and especially note 60.

ited in fact, then it must be granted that he who is now among the number of the predestinate has always been among their number and that the previously posited number was not the number of the predestinate, but that another, greater number [was the number of the predestinate]. From the fact that a *de possibili* proposition is posited in fact [it follows that] every proposition inconsistent with it is to be denied, just as from the fact that 'it is possible that Socrates is seated' is posited in fact [it follows that] 'Socrates is standing' must be denied.[88]

J   [*Part Four*]

It is argued that whoever does not know a contingent proposition *A* and can know *A* can begin to know *A*, for it does not seem that an affirmation is true after a denial—[i.e.,] after [the affirmation] was not true—unless it begins to be true. Therefore if He does not know the proposition *A* and can know *A* [His knowledge] can change.

I maintain that if you understand *A* to be a contingent proposition about the present, the proposition [that whoever does not know a contingent proposition *A* and can know *A* can begin to know *A*] is true, and in that case I grant the conclusion that God can begin to know *A*. But the further conclusion that [His knowledge] changes does not follow, as is clear above.[89]

If, however, you understand *A* to be a contingent proposition about the future, the proposition [that whoever does not know *A* and can know *A* can begin to know *A*] is not true, for its being true requires that the two propositions 'God does not know *A*' and 'God does know *A*' be true successively, and they cannot be true successively. For just as nothing is known by God unless it is true, so also everything true is known by God, and therefore if *A* is true it always was true and hence always was known by God. Therefore, furthermore, 'God does not know *A*' was never true. Consequently the conclusion 'God can begin to know *A*' does not follow, for it would never follow unless first 'God does not know *A*' and after that 'God does know *A*' were true.

[88]Cf. Book One of Ockham's *Commentary on the Sentences* (the *Ordinatio*), d. 39, q. u. (Appendix I, pp. 92–95 below), where Ockham considers the question "whether God can know more than He knows" in a discussion closely paralleling the one in Question II, Article III, Parts Two and Three of this treatise.

[89]Question II, Article III, Part One.

K   *[Part Five]*

[It is argued that] if God does not know *A* and can know *A* [then if He does know *A*] it will be through [His] intellect. Thus there is a natural active power in it. But such [a power] cannot act after having not acted without there being a change. Therefore God changes.[90]

I maintain[91] that the proposition 'a natural power cannot act [after having not acted without there being a change]' is true whenever the propositions 'such a power is not acting' and 'such a power is acting' can be verified successively, and otherwise not. Thus if 'God does not understand *A*'[92] (where *A* is a future contingent) and 'God does understand *A*' could be true successively, it would follow that God is mutable, for [the immutability of His knowledge] could not be preserved through the change of the future contingent. But that [future contingent] cannot change from falsity to truth so that it is first false and afterwards true. For, as has often been said, even if it is posited that God does not understand *A* because *A* is false and can be true, if it is posited in fact that *A* is true, then 'God does understand *A*' is true and always was true. Consequently 'God does

---

[90]Since the expected conclusion is 'God's knowledge can change,' the stated conclusion is likely to seem unwarrantedly strong. In one sense it is so; the argument plainly does not support '. . . changes' rather than '. . . can change.' But since God's knowledge is an aspect of God's essence, the conclusion 'God can change' is not *prima facie* unwarranted. Notice that in his reply Ockham takes that conclusion — "God is mutable" — to have been the one intended. (All this suggests that "*igitur Deus mutatur*" may be a scribe's error for "*igitur Deus mutabilis*," but the notes to Boehner's edition indicate no variant readings for this passage.)

[91]In the first three sentences of this reply we have twice reversed the order of affirmative and negative propositions and twice reversed the order of claims about truth and falsity. These changes are required in order (1) to align the reply with the argument to which it is directed, (2) to bring the beginning of the reply into agreement with its concluding sentences, and (3) to make Ockham's claims about the truth and falsity of future contingents in this reply consistent with his other observations on this topic. Without these changes the first three sentences of Ockham's reply would read as follows: "I maintain that the proposition 'a natural power cannot act [after having not acted without there being a change]' is true whenever the propositions 'such a power is acting' and 'such a power is not acting' can be verified successively, and otherwise not. Thus if 'God does understand *A*' (where *A* is a future contingent) and 'God does not understand *A*' could be true successively, it would follow that God is mutable, for [the immutability of His knowledge] could not be preserved through the change of the future contingent, since that [future contingent] cannot change from truth to falsity so that it is first true and afterwards false."

[92]Ockham's use of such expressions as 'God understands *A*' (*Deus intelligit A*) and 'God knows A' (*Deus scit A*) may be open to misunderstanding, in the former case more than in the latter. Suppose that the proposition replacing '*A*' is 'Socrates will sit

not understand *A*' always was false, since if one part of a contradiction always was true the other always was false, and vice versa.

[Article IV]⁹³

L   Fourth, it is argued that God does have necessary knowledge regarding future contingents.⁹⁴

[Part One]

For this follows: God knows *A* immutably; therefore necessarily. Proof of the inference: Necessity is not posited in God except for the necessity that belongs to immutability; therefore whatever is in Him immutably is in Him necessarily.

I maintain that ['God does have necessary knowledge regarding future contingents'] can be understood in two ways. [Understood] in the first way [it means] that* God's knowledge whereby future contingents are known is necessary. And this is true, since the divine essence itself is one single necessary and immutable cognition of all things, complexes as well as non-complexes, necessary and contingent. [Understood] in the second way [it means] that by that knowledge future contingents are known necessarily. And in that way [His knowledge] is not necessary, nor need it be granted that God has necessary knowledge regarding future contingents; instead, [His knowledge regarding them] is contingent. For just as this or that future contingent contingently will be, so God knows that it contingently will be, for if He knows it He can *not* know that it will be.⁹⁵

---

down.' What is meant by those expressions is, of course, that God understands that Socrates will sit down, or that God understands that 'Socrates will sit down' is true, and not that God understands the proposition 'Socrates will sit down' (and similarly for 'knows').

⁹³Cf. Duns Scotus, *Opus Oxoniense*, I, d. 39, q. u., n. 5 (ed. Vivès, t. 10, p. 614) and n. 31 (p. 653). Cf. Book One of Ockham's *Commentary on the Sentences* (the *Ordinatio*), d. 38, q. 1, N (against "certain scholars"). [Appendix I, pp. 90–91 below.] (Boehner)

⁹⁴In Articles I, II, and III the opening arguments attacked the ascription of the property in question to God's knowledge and Ockham's replies defended it. In Article IV, on the *necessity* of God's knowledge regarding future contingents, the opening arguments of each of the five parts defend the ascription of the property while Ockham's replies attack it.

⁹⁵The expected (and probably the intended) wording of the second clause of

Next, in reply to the argument, I maintain that the inference does not hold good. For although [God's] knowledge is immutable and the object known—viz., a future contingent—is immutable in such a way that it cannot be first true and afterwards false[96] (as has often been said), still it does not follow that necessarily God knows it, but rather contingently. For although A itself cannot change from truth to falsity or vice versa, it is nevertheless contingent, and so it can be false and consequently not known by God. Thus contingently it is known by God and not necessarily. Therefore there is a fallacy of the consequent there [in the argument], for it follows the other way around but not this way. Similarly, there is a fallacy of the consequent here: 'A cannot be first true and afterwards false; therefore it cannot be false,' for it follows the other way around but not this way.

As for the proof of the inference, I grant that there is no necessity in God except for the necessity that belongs to immutability, for other kinds of necessity—e.g., the necessity of compulsion (*coactionis*)—are not posited in God because [they entail] imperfection. Thus the inference 'something necessary is in God; therefore something immutable' follows correctly, but not the other way around, for everything necessary is immutable and not vice versa, unless one is speaking of those immutables that are God Himself. For many complexes are known by God [to be] immutable which are nevertheless not necessary but simply contingent.

---

this sentence is "so God knows contingently that it will be," but the Latin is "*ita Deus scit ipsum contingenter fore*" (rather than ". . . *scit contingenter ipsum* . . ."). Ockham is of course not claiming that God is only contingently and not necessarily omniscient. The issue here is not whether His knowing all true propositions is a necessary property of His but whether His knowing this or that proposition in particular is a necessary property of His. Since the proposition in question is a true *contingent*, it is possible that it not be true, and hence possible that it not be known by God, and hence not necessary that it be known by God. Cf. *Tractatus de Principiis Theologiae* (ed. L. Baudry, "Études de Philosophie Médiévale," XXIII; Paris, Librairie Philosophique J. Vrin, 1936), [105], where Ockham's reply to the objector is explained with admirable clarity by the compiler of this compendium of Ockham's views.

[96]Because a future contingent is at issue here it seems incorrect or at best misleading to say without qualification that "it cannot be first true and afterwards false." If 'Socrates will sit down at t_n' is true now, then at t_n and ever afterwards it will be false (see, e.g., p. 62). But the kind of revision that seemed appropriate in similar circumstances in Ockham's reply to the opening argument in Part Five of Article III (see note 91) is not appropriate here, since Ockham is speaking of future contingents that are known by God and hence about such as are now true. This reply must therefore be read with the understanding that the change of truth-value is being considered only during all time prior to t_n. See note 16.

M   *[Part Two]*

It is argued that everything possible is mutable; therefore everything immutable is necessary. But God's knowledge is immutable. Therefore [God's knowledge is necessary]. Alternatively, this is mutable; therefore it is contingent. Therefore, similarly, this is immutable; therefore it is necessary—by this rule: if what is opposed to one thing may be inferred from what is opposed to another, then the one thing may be inferred from the other (*si oppositum de opposito, et propositum de proposito*).

In reply to the second argument* I maintain that the inference does not hold good. As for the rule, I say that it has to be understood [to apply only] when one argues from the opposite of the consequent to the opposite of the antecedent. But the argument here is the other way around, and thus there is a fallacy of the consequent.

N   *[Part Three]*

[It is argued that] whatever can be in God, of necessity is God, since He is immutable. But knowing *A* can be in God. Therefore necessarily it is in God. Therefore necessarily He knows *A*.

I maintain that that which is in God or can be in Him formally, necessarily is God. Knowing *A* is not in God formally, however, but merely through predication; for it is a certain concept or name that is [sometimes] predicated of God and at other times not. And it is not necessary that it be God, for the name 'Lord' is predicated of God contingently and temporally and nevertheless is not God.[97]

O   *[Part Four]*

[It is argued that] every absolute perfection is in God necessarily, but knowing *A* is of this sort; therefore [knowing *A* is in God necessarily]. The minor premiss is proved as follows: God would not be perfect if He did not know *A*, for He is not imperfect except as a result of the lack of some absolute perfection; therefore necessarily He knows *A*.

I maintain that 'absolute perfection' is sometimes used for the perfection which is God, to which no perfection can be added, and knowing *A* is not an absolute perfection in this sense, for [knowing

---

[97]Article IV, Part Three bears some resemblance to Question I, Objection 5 (see pp. 41–42). On 'Lord' see Article IV, Part Four (p. 70).

A] is a concept or an utterance.[98] At other times it is used for some concept from the negation of which with respect to something it follows that that thing is imperfect, and so knowing A is not an absolute perfection in this sense either. For 'God does not know A; therefore God is imperfect' does not follow, since if A is false, God does not know A.

Suppose it is said that 'God does not know A and A is true; therefore God is imperfect' does follow. I grant that if both premisses are true the conclusion does follow. But from the truth of the first premiss alone no imperfection in God follows. Still, that is what is required if [knowing A] is to be an absolute perfection. For example, from the truth of the two propositions 'God is not the Lord' and 'Man is a servant' it does follow that there is an imperfection in God — viz., that He is not the Lord of every servant. But from the first proposition alone no imperfection follows, for if we suppose that there are no creatures, 'God is not the Lord; therefore He is imperfect' does not follow.

P   [*Part Five*]

[It is argued that] everything that God knows will be, necessarily will be, and A is something that God knows will be; therefore necessarily A will be. The major premiss is a *de necessario* [proposition], since the predicate necessarily inheres in the subject. The minor premiss is omnitemporally assertoric, since it is true for eternity. Therefore a *de necessario* conclusion follows.

I maintain that the major premiss is false, since it expresses the sense of division, and many things that God knows will be, contingently will be and not necessarily. Therefore a false conclusion follows. If, on the other hand, the major premiss is taken in the sense of composition — so that 'everything that God knows will be will be' is necessary — then the mixed inference does not hold good, for the minor premiss is temporally assertoric, and so the conclusion does not follow.[99]

[98]The phrase "a concept or an utterance" is evidently an abbreviated version of the expression Ockham used towards the end of Part Three: "a certain concept or name that is sometimes predicated of God and at other times not."

[99]The technical terminology in Part Five may need some explanation. On "*de necessario*" propositions see note 37. On "mixed inference" and "omnitemporally" or "temporally" assertoric propositions see note 72. On the senses of division and of composition see note 60. Ockham specifically discusses mixed inferences involving assertoric propositions and *de necessario* propositions in *Summa logicae*, III (1), c. 31–c. 33 (ed. Boehner, pp. 402–414).

[QUESTION III]^{100}

A   How can the contingency of the will, both created and uncreated, be preserved in [the case of its] causing something external? That is, can the will, as naturally prior to the caused act, cause the opposite act at the same instant at which it causes that act, or can it at another, subsequent instant cause the opposite act or cease from that caused act?

     Scotus maintains^{101} that in the created will there is a double

---

^{100}Question III is the most difficult of the five Questions in the *Treatise*. Some of its specific difficulties will be discussed in other notes, but because even its organization is more difficult than that of the other Questions we supply the following outline (in terms of marginal letters and paragraphs).

(A) Par. 1.   The posing of the question
        Par. 2.   A presentation of Scotus's answer to the question, centering around Scotus's doctrine of a "nonevident capacity" of the will
(B) Par. 3.   Ockham's initial attempt to reduce that doctrine to an absurdity
        Par. 4.   An objection to Par. 3
        Par. 5.   Ockham's reply to Par. 4
(C) Par. 6.   Ockham's revised attempt to reduce Scotus's doctrine to an absurdity, based on Par. 5
        Par. 7.   Ockham's reply to a remark in Par. 4 intended to assimilate his own treatment of future contingents to the present discussion
        Par. 8.   An attempt to show that an example introduced in Par. 2 leads to an absurdity in the absence of Scotus's doctrine
        Par. 9.   Ockham's reply to Par. 8
        Par. 10.   A simpler version of the argument in Par. 8
        Par. 11.   Ockham's reply to Par. 10
(D) Par. 12.   Ockham's explicit rejection of Scotus's doctrine of the "nonevident capacity"
        Par. 13.   A question challenging Ockham to show how his own view preserves the contingency of the will
        Par. 14.   Ockham's reply to Par. 13, consisting mainly in his distinction of three senses of 'the will acts contingently at the instant at which it acts.'

^{101}In *Opus Oxoniense*, I, d. 39, q. u., nn. 16 ff. (ed. Vivès, t. 10, p. 628). Cf. Book One of Ockham's *Commentary on the Sentences* (the *Ordinatio*), d. 38, q. 1, **B** and **E** [Appendix I, pp. 81–82 and 85 below]. (Boehner)

capacity for opposites. The one is evident and is a capacity for opposite objects or for opposite acts in succession, so that [a created will] can will something at t_1 and not will it or will against it at t_2. The other is a nonevident capacity, which is for opposites without succession.[102] For it is imagined [by Scotus] that at one and the same instant of time there is more than one instant of nature. And in that case if there were now a created will that only remained through one instant and at that time willed some object contingently, that will itself, as naturally prior to that volition, has a capacity for the opposite act at[103] the same instant of duration at which that [willed] act is posited, so that, as naturally prior, it can will against that [willed act] at that instant.[104] And so this capacity is called nonevident, for it is a capacity for opposite acts at one and the same instant of time without any succession.

B   Against that opinion it is argued as follows.* That capacity which can be actualized by no power is not a real capacity and

---

[102]"The will has a capacity for opposites without succession' is ambiguous. It can be taken to mean that (1) at a single time the will can will X and the will can *not* will X (or will not-X). (A will with such a capacity is evidently one that acts contingently in the first sense distinguished by Ockham in the concluding paragraph of Question III, p. 76.) On the other hand, it can be taken to mean that (2) at a single time the will can will X and not will X (or will not-X). (A will with such a capacity would evidently be one that acted contingently in the impossible second sense distinguished by Ockham, p. 76.) Ockham construes Scotus's doctrine as involving interpretation (2). His reasons for doing so may be connected with his rejection of Scotus's "instants of nature" (see notes 49 and 104 and Introduction, pp. 31–32). But in at least one passage in his *Opus Oxoniense* (I, d. 39, Appendix A) Scotus takes account of such an ambiguity and rejects an interpretation analogous to this interpretation (2). " 'A will willing a can *not* will a.' This . . . [proposition] is false in the sense of composition, since what is signified [in that sense] is the possibility of the composition 'a will willing a does not will a.' It is true in the sense of division, since what is signified [in that sense] is a possibility for opposites successively, since a will willing for a can *not* will for b." (Quoted in Latin by Bernardine M. Bonansea in "Duns Scotus' Voluntarism" [pp. 83–121 in *John Duns Scotus, 1265–1965*, ed. J. K. Ryan and B. M. Bonansea; Studies in Philosophy and the History of Philosophy, Vol. 3; Washington, D.C., Catholic University of America Press, 1965], p. 89, n. 24.)

[103]The Latin preposition usually occurring in such phrases is 'in': 'in A instanti' ('at t_1'), 'in eodem instanti' ('at the same instant'). But here and at several other points in Question III Ockham uses 'pro' instead of 'in.' This difference of course suggests the possibility of a distinction to be taken account of in the translation, but a survey of all such uses in Question III indicates that the difference is random and does not affect the sense. Since alternating between such English prepositions as 'at' and 'for' would suggest a difference in senses, we use 'at' for both 'in' and 'pro' in such time phrases.

[104]The notion of natural priority alluded to here stems from Aristotle's *Categories* Ch. 12, 14b12: "For of things which reciprocate as to implication of existence,

is not to be really posited. This nonevident capacity is of that kind. Therefore [this nonevident capacity is not a real capacity and is not to be really posited]. The minor premiss is proved as follows. If so [i.e., if this nonevident capacity can be actualized by some power], then [suppose that] 'the will wills X' is true at t_1. But it can be actualized by you at the same instant in respect of not willing. Therefore at one and the same instant 'the will wills X' and 'the will does not will X' would be true together, and so contradictories will be true at one and the same time.[105]

Suppose that it is said that if [this nonevident capacity] *is* actualized so that 'the will does not will X at t_1' is true, then its opposite 'the will wills X at t_1' is false[106] (just as, according to you, although 'Peter will be saved' is true now, if it is posited that Peter is damned then 'God does not will supreme blessedness for Peter' is true).

On the contrary: every proposition that is merely about the present, if it is true, has [corresponding to it] a necessary proposition about the past. But by hypothesis 'the will wills X at t_1' is true, and it is merely about the present. Therefore 'the will willed X at t_1' will be necessary forever after. Therefore after t_1 'the will did not will X at t_1' cannot be true. This is confirmed as follows. If after t_1 'the will willed X at t_1' was always necessary, then after t_1 its opposite was always impossible; further, then after t_1 it always was and will

---

that which is in some way the cause of the other's existence might reasonably be called prior by nature." Ockham evidently has no quarrel with this notion but rejects Scotus's analysis of natural priority in terms of instants of nature (see p. 76), apparently because of the absurdities entailed by the supposition that there *are* such instants of nature. (See Baudry, *Lexique*, art. "*Instans naturae*.") But Scotus's analysis of natural priority seems to have been modeled on the conventional analysis of temporal priority in terms of instants of time, and it need not be interpreted as committing him to the reality of instants of nature any more than the conventional analysis of temporal priority need be interpreted as committing one to the reality of instants of time. (See note 49 and Appendix I, note 7.)

[105]Ockham produces a parallel argument against Scotus's doctrine of the "nonevident capacity" in his *Ordinatio*, d. 38, q. u. **E** (Appendix I, p. 85 below).

[106]This objection is evidently intended to reject Ockham's attempted reduction to an absurdity in the preceding paragraph by claiming flatly that an actualization of the nonevident capacity would be an actualization for the one opposite or for the other, and that an actualization for either one would simply rule out an actualization for the other at the same time. That is, this objection seems to be following the line laid down as interpretation (1) in note 102. A parallel objection appears in Ockham's *Ordinatio* (immediately following the passage cited in note 105; Appendix I, p. 85 below).

be true to say that 'the will does not will X'[107] could not have been true at t_1, since at that time its opposite was true — viz., 'the will wills* X at t_1.'[108]

C   The response, therefore, consists in this. If the will wills X at t_1, then after t_1 'the will willed X at t_1' always will be necessary. And in that case if its nonevident capacity can be actualized at t_1, then either contradictories will be true at one and the same time after t_1, or after t_1 that proposition which is necessary about the past (since it had [corresponding to it] a true proposition that was merely about the present) will be false, for its opposite will be true.

Nor does that objection hold good in which it is said ". . . 'Peter will be saved' is true now . . .," for that is a future contingent, and in the case of future contingents the aforesaid proposition has no truth — viz.,* 'every proposition that is [merely] about the present, [if it is true, has corresponding to it a necessary proposition about the past].'

But you say: According to you, an angel can sin at the first instant of his creation.[109] Then [you go on] as follows. One never sins except at an instant at which the sinner has his act in his power, so that he can at that same instant not elicit that act. For grant the opposite — that he cannot at that instant not elicit that act — and, since 'not possible not' is equipollent to 'necessary,' it follows that at that instant necessarily he elicits that act and so does not sin.[110]

I respond as follows. On the hypothesis [that an angel can sin

---

[107]Reading *non vult hoc* for *non vult hoc oppositum.*

[108]Ockham produces a parallel argument in his *Ordinatio* (immediately following the passage cited in note 106; Appendix I, p. 85 below).

[109]The first sentence of this objection presents two difficulties, the first of which is the use of the second-person verb form and pronoun in what seems to be a direct quotation: "*Sed dicis: Angelus secundum te in primo instanti suae creationis potest peccare.*" It looks as if Ockham is the speaker and is quoting an objector, in which case the 'you' in 'you say' refers to the objector and the 'you' in 'according to you' refers to Ockham. In the second sentence, then, Ockham is again the speaker, and the remainder of the paragraph is a quotation from the objector. The second difficulty is the unexpected reference to an angel. It seems that the objector has in mind the example Ockham used in his presentation of Scotus's view (in the second paragraph of this Question). Since the example was of a created will existing for only one instant and capable of willing in that first (and last) instant of its existence, an angel's will is certainly a more suitable instance than the will of a human being.

[110]The point of the objection seems to be to show that Ockham's rejection of Scotus's nonevident capacity of the will for opposites *without succession* commits him to admitting that a will that exists for a single instant only (or, more generally, every will at the first instant of its operation) *must* will as it does.

at the first instant of his creation] I maintain that he does have the act in his power, since he can cease [from eliciting the act] at another instant, so that at one instant 'the will wills [X]' is true and at another instant 'the will does not will [X]' is true. I maintain also that he can at t_1 not elicit that act, for when t_1 is past 'the will can at t_1 not elicit that act' is true, since after t_1 it can cease from [eliciting] any act, and then t_1 is past and then 'the will does not elicit that act at t_1' is true.[111]

Suppose it is said that when it is t_1 and an act is elicited [at t_1] the will cannot not elicit that act, and therefore (by equipollence) at t_1 it necessarily elicits [that act].

I maintain that the inference does not hold good, since, following the teaching of the Philosopher,[112] the equipollence must be understood [to apply] in absolute propositions with no assumption having been made.[113] (Otherwise many absurd conclusions would follow against the Philosopher.)

D   Therefore, responding to this Question [III] in another way, I maintain that in creatures there is never a capacity for opposite objects* or for opposite acts without succession, nor in divine [beings a capacity] in respect of those that are not future contingents.[114] And so I do not agree with Scotus* as regards that nonevi-

---

[111]As it stands the last sentence of Ockham's reply seems so obviously mistaken as to suggest that the text is corrupt at this point. Nothing in Boehner's edition or his notes on variants provides any textual basis for an emendation; nevertheless, we propose the following (requiring only the change of an occasional 'A' in the Latin text to a 'B'). "I maintain also that he can at t_2 not elicit that act, for when t_1 is past 'the will can at t_2 not elicit that act' is true, since after t_1 it can cease from [eliciting] any act, and then t_1 is past and then 'the will does not elicit that act at t_2' is true." Even with this emendation, however, Ockham's reply seems inadequate, for it establishes only that the angel's will is contingent in sense (3) (p. 76), and contingency in sense (3) is compatible with strict determinism. Contingency in sense (1)—i.e., freedom of the will—is a necessary condition of sinning.

[112]See Aristotle's table of equipollent modal expressions in *De interpretatione*, Ch. 13, 22a25–32, also Chs. 12 and 13 generally.

[113]The objector's inference may be represented as follows: "If p, then it is not possible that not p. 'Not possible . . . not' is equipollent to 'necessary.' Therefore if p, then it is necessary that p." What Ockham says in rejecting this inference evidently amounts to noting that the modal expressions are misplaced. With the modal expressions placed justifiably the inference would lose the point intended by the objector. "It is not possible that if p then not p. 'Not possible . . . not' is equipollent to 'necessary.' Therefore it is necessary that if p then p."

[114]Ockham is assuming that 'God wills Peter to be saved' is a future contingent proposition if it is construed as a claim about God's consequent disposing will, but

dent capacity in the will, for he is mistaken in all those "instants of nature."

But how then will the contingency of the will be preserved in respect of what is willed by it?

I answer that God's will (as regards what is external to it), as well as the created will, acts contingently at the instant at which it acts. But this can be understood in three ways. (1) [It can be understood to mean] that the will, existing for some time prior to t_1, at which time it causes [X], can freely and contingently cause or not cause [X] at t_1. Understood in this way, it is true if the will does thus preexist. (2) It can be understood [to mean] that at the same instant at which the will causes [X] it is true to say that it does not cause [X]. Understood in this way it is not possible, because of the contradictories that follow — viz., that it causes [X] at t_1 and does not cause [X] at t_1. (3) It can be understood [to mean] that the will contingently causes [X] at t_1, for without any variation or change occurring in it or in another cause and without the cessation of another cause it can at another instant, after t_1, freely cease from [causing] its act, so that at t_1 'the will causes [X]' is true and at another instant, after t_1, 'the will does not cause [X]' is true. And in this way the will does contingently cause [X] at t_1, but a natural cause does not contingently cause in this way.[115]

---

not if it is construed as a claim about God's antecedent disposing will. (On this distinction see Introduction, pp. 17–20, 30–33 above.) But propositions about present acts of a created will are settled as regards their truth or falsity by what is posited in actuality in the present. They are thus like propositions about God's antecedent will and unlike propositions about God's consequent will. A proposition about God's consequent willing that p is equivalent to a future contingent proposition in case it is future and contingent that p.

[115]Cf. Baudry, *Lexique*, art. "*Contingentia*."

[QUESTION IV][116]

A   Is there a cause of predestination in the predestinate and a cause of reprobation in the reprobate?

It is proved that there is no cause of predestination [in the predestinate], since baptized infants are saved although they never earned merit (*habuerunt merita*).[117] Therefore [in at least some predestinate persons there is no cause of predestination]. Again, in the predestinate angels it does not seem that merit precedes [predestination]. Therefore [in at least some (other) predestinate persons there is no cause of predestination].

B   I maintain that there is a cause of predestination in the predestinate and of reprobation in the reprobate as long as 'cause' is being taken in the second rather than in the first way mentioned in Assumption 9. For this inference is correct: 'He commits the sin of final impenitence;[118] therefore he will be reprobate.' Similarly: 'He will persevere to the end; therefore he will be predestinate.' For just as God is not a punisher before a man is a sinner, so He is not a rewarder before a man is justified by grace.

Nevertheless, I maintain as well that a cause of reprobation (or of predestination) can precede [reprobation (or predestination)] in the reprobate (or predestinate) or in [his] parents. For instance, an infant dying in original sin is punished with the penalty of damnation (*poena damni*) because of the sin of the parents, but not with the penalty of bodily suffering (*poena sensus*) unless because of his own sins. Similarly, a baptized child can be saved and hence predestinate because of the good works of the parents.*

The cause of predestination may, however, admit of an exception in the Blessed Virgin and in the good angels if they did not merit their supreme blessedness. If, on the other hand, they did finally merit it, it does not admit of an exception.

And thus [my response] to the two arguments is plain.

[116]Cf. Duns Scotus, *Opus Oxoniense*, I, d. 41, q. u., nn. 11 ff. (ed. Vivès, t. 10, pp. 697 ff.); also Book One of Ockham's *Commentary on the Sentences* (the *Ordinatio*), d. 40, q. 1. (Boehner)

[117]See note 12.

[118]See note 4.

77

[QUESTION V]

A   In view of the fact that the propositions 'Peter is predestinate' and 'Peter is reprobate'* are opposites, why cannot the one
succeed the other in truth?[119]

I maintain that, as is clear from the preceding [discussions], if
those propositions are simply about the future, not conveying anything present posited in fact or anything past, then they cannot
be successively verified unless 'Peter is predestinate' is first true and
afterwards false; but that is impossible. For, as has been said above,
every proposition that is simply about the future was always true if
it is ever true;[120] for there is no reason why it should be true at one
time rather than at another. Consequently, since propositions such
as 'Peter is predestinate' are equivalently simply about the future, if
those propositions can be verified successively and it is certain that
they cannot be true at one and the same time (since they entail that
contradictories are true at one and the same time[121]) then if 'Peter
is reprobate' is true now it was always true earlier,[122] since it is simply about the future. Consequently it was true when its opposite
was true, and so contradictories were true at one and the same
time.

This is confirmed as follows. Propositions do not change from
truth to falsity except as a result of a change on the part of a thing,
according to the Philosopher in *Categories* [Ch. 5, 4a22 ff.]. But
there is no change in God or in Peter or in anything else as a result
of which 'Peter is predestinate' is first true and afterwards false. (I

---

[119]Question V is devoted to an elucidation and defense of two principles fundamental to Ockham's position in this treatise: (1) that such propositions as 'Peter is
predestinate' and 'Peter is reprobate' are "simply about the future, not conveying
anything present posited in fact or anything past"; (2) that a proposition that is
simply about the future is "always true [prior to the time of its realization] if it is ever
true."

[120]See pp. 61–62.

[121]Speaking strictly, it is not they but their being true together that entails that
contradictories are true at one and the same time.

[122]Reading '*prius*' for '*postea*.'

say this with the understanding that the proposition is simply about the future and [is under consideration only] prior to the granting of supreme blessedness.) The following example is analogous. If 'you will sit down tomorrow' is true now there is no change occurring in you or in anything else as a result of which you[123] can* make that proposition false before tomorrow, so that it would be true to say [before tomorrow] that the proposition 'you will sit down tomorrow' was true earlier and is false now. Therefore it is impossible that the propositions ['Peter is predestinate' and 'Peter is reprobate'] change in that way from truth to falsity or vice versa.*

B   Suppose you say that if you die today then 'you will sit down tomorrow' is false and was true of you earlier, and that as a result of such a change in you that proposition can change from truth to falsity. And in the same way if Peter is now predestinate and afterwards dies in final impenitence he will then be reprobate. Therefore as a result of a change occurring in Peter through an act of sin the proposition 'Peter is predestinate' can change from truth to falsity.

In that case I maintain that (as has often been said) if it is posited that someone predestinate commits the sin of final impenitence, then 'he is reprobate' is true and 'he is reprobate' always was true and consequently its opposite is now false and always was false. And in the same way if you die today the proposition 'you will sit down tomorrow' is now false and always was false and its opposite always was true.

And the entire difficulty in the subject-matter [of predestination, God's foreknowledge, and future contingents] might be said to rest on this response.[124]

---

[123]Boehner conjectures that the word 'Deus' was inadvertently omitted at this point and reads *potest Deus* rather than *potes*.

[124]The following closing formulas are found in various manuscripts of the *Treatise*. "Amen. Here ends the treatise on future contingents and divine predestination set forth by brother William Ockham, O.F.M." "Here ends the treatise on predestination and future contingents of the reverend brother William Ockham, O.F.M. Praise be to God." "Here ends Ockham's treatise on predestination and future contingents." "Here ends the treatise on predestination and foreknowledge or on future contingents set forth by the venerable brother William Ockham, professor of Holy Scripture, O.F.M." (Boehner)

APPENDICES

APPENDIX I

Ordinatio,[1] Distinctions 38 and 39

Distinction 38

A   Regarding the thirty-eighth distinction I ask whether God has determinate and necessary knowledge of all future contingents.

[It seems] that He does not. For that which is not determinately true in itself is determinately true for no one, but a future contingent is not determinately true in itself; therefore [a future contingent is determinately true for no one]. Consequently it is not determinately true for God. Then I argue as follows.[2] That which is not determinately true is not known by God with determinate knowledge, but a future contingent is of that sort, as has been shown; therefore [a future contingent is not known by God with determinate knowledge].

It seems, moreover, that He does not have necessary knowl-

---

[1]A scholastic treatise deriving from a course of lectures may be a *reportatio*, a transcript of notes taken by someone other than the author of the lectures, or an *ordinatio*, the author's own version, often a revision and expansion of the original lectures. Book One of Ockham's *Commentary on the Sentences* of Peter Lombard is an *ordinatio* and is often cited in the literature as "the *Ordinatio*," as here. The other three books of the Commentary have survived as a *reportatio*.

[2]The "I" of this paragraph and the next is not Ockham but an objector.

edge [of all future contingents]. For if He has necessary knowledge of some future contingent, *A*, then I argue as follows. God has necessary knowledge of *A*; therefore 'God knows *A*' is necessary. Further, therefore '*A* is true' is necessary. But if '*A* is true' is necessary, *A* is not contingent. Consequently, *A* is not a future contingent, which is counter to the hypothesis.

On the contrary, "all things are naked and open to His eyes"[3]; therefore all things are known by God. But nothing is known except with determinate knowledge. Therefore God has determinate knowledge of all things.

Again, it seems that He has necessary knowledge. For there is one single knowledge (*unica scientia*) in God; therefore God's knowledge of necessaries and of contingents is one and the same. But God's knowledge of necessaries is necessary; therefore God's knowledge of future contingents is necessary. Consequently God has necessary knowledge of contingents.

B   Regarding the question[4] it is said that although it cannot be proved *a priori*, it must nevertheless be maintained that there are future contingents.

On this supposition [viz., that there are future contingents], it is said that contingency in things can be preserved only if the first cause, which acts through the [divine] intellect and will, causes contingently — and this while perfect causality is posited in the first [cause],[5] as Catholics posit it. Thus this contingency must be sought either in the divine intellect or in the divine will. But not in the divine intellect, because whatever the intellect understands it understands merely naturally.[6] Consequently it must be sought in the divine will. He [Scotus] says that in order to understand this (*ad cuius*

---

[3]*Hebrews* 4:13 (Boehner).

[4]Boehner supplies (in Latin) the following subtitle for the text from marginal letter **B** to marginal letter **E**: "Regarding the Question. Duns Scotus's View, *Opus Oxoniense*, Book I, d. 39."

[5]Reading '*in prima*' for '*in primo*.'

[6]Ockham is evidently alluding here to what he elsewhere calls "the possible intellect." "The agent intellect and the possible intellect are altogether the same in reality and in reason. Nevertheless these names or concepts rightly connote different things. For 'the agent intellect' signifies the soul while connoting intellection *proceeding from* the active soul, while 'the possible intellect' signifies that same soul while connoting intellection *received in* the soul. But [the soul] is altogether the same both effecting and receiving intellection" (Book Two of his *Commentary on the Sentences*, q. 24 **Q** [in Baudry, *Lexique*, art. "*Intellectus*."]) In the case of the divine intellect, however, it is difficult to see how even that sort of distinction could be maintained.

intellectum) one must see, first, in relation to what things our will is free, and second, in what way possibility or contingency follows from that freedom.

As to the first point, it is said that the will, insofar as it is first actuality,[7] is free as regards opposite acts; and by means of those opposite acts it is free as regards opposite objects, which it intends; and further, [it is free] as regards opposite effects, which it produces. The first freedom necessarily has a certain imperfection associated with it—viz., the passive potentiality and mutability of the will. The second freedom, however, is without any imperfection, even if the will cannot have the third freedom.

C   Regarding the second point, it is said that an evident capacity for opposites accompanies that [first] freedom. For although there is no capacity for willing and not willing at one and the same time (for that is nothing at all), nevertheless there is in [the will] a capacity for willing after not willing, or for a succession of opposite acts.

In [connection with] these [opposite acts], however, there is another [capacity], not evident in this way, [and] without any succession. For if we suppose that there is a created will that exists at only one instant, and that at that instant it has this or that volition, then it does not necessarily have it at first. For if at that instant it had the volition necessarily (since it is a cause only at that instant when it caused the volition), then, absolutely, the will, when it caused the volition, would cause it necessarily. For it is not now a contingent cause because it pre-existed before the instant at which it causes and pre-existing then could either cause or not cause. For just as this or that being, when it is, is then either necessary or contingent, so a cause, when it causes, causes then either necessarily or contingently. Therefore whatever this willing causes at that instant, and causes not necessarily, it causes contingently. Therefore this capacity to cause the opposite of that which it does cause is without succession. And this real capacity is a naturally prior capacity (as of first actuality) for opposites—[opposites] that are naturally posterior (as of second actuality). For first actuality, considered at that

---

[7]The will is first actuality (or is in a state of first actualization) considered as a real capacity for action. The realization of that capacity in action is second actuality. First actuality is conceived of *as if* temporally prior to second actuality. See Wolter, *Duns Scotus: Philosophical Writings*, pp. 57–58. See also *Treatise*, nn. 49 and 104 above.

instant at which it is, is naturally prior to second actuality. Thus [first actuality] contingently posits [second actuality] in reality as its effect, so that as naturally prior it could equally posit the opposite in reality.

On the basis of these remarks some things are said about the divine will.

First, what its freedom is. And it is said that the divine will is not free as regards the distinct acts of willing and willing against. But because of the limitlessness of volition [the divine will] is free as regards opposite objects, and that is [its] first [freedom]. In addition to that there is a freedom as regards opposite effects, and the divine will is free [in that respect] insofar as it is operative, not insofar as it is productive or receptive of its volition.

Second, in relation to what things the divine will is free. And it is said that it relates necessarily to no object but its own essence. Therefore it relates contingently to anything else, so that it can be [related] to the opposite – and this while it is considered as naturally prior intending the object, not only as the will is naturally prior to its act, but also insofar as it is willing [its act]. For our will, as naturally prior to its act, elicits that act in such a way that it could at one and the same instant elicit its opposite. In the same way the divine will, insofar as volition itself alone is naturally prior to such an intention (*tendentia*), intends the object contingently in such a way that at the same instant it could intend the opposite object. And this [is] as much by virtue of a logical capacity – i.e., the compatibility (*non-repugnantia*) of the terms (as he said earlier regarding our will) – as by virtue of the real capacity – i.e., [the will's being] naturally prior to its act.

D   But how is the certainty of the divine knowledge consistent with such contingency? It is said that this can be posited in two ways.

In one way by this means, that the divine intellect seeing the determination of the divine will sees that x will be at t_1, since the will determines that it will be at t_1; for [the divine intellect] knows that the will is immutable and unimpedable.

He [Scotus] says that it can be posited in another way. For the divine intellect either presents [to itself] simples, the union of which is contingent in reality; or if it presents to itself complexity, it presents it as neutral with respect to itself, and the will choosing one part — viz., a conjunction of these [simples] for something [that is] now in reality[8] — makes 'x will be at t_1' determinately true. Insofar as this exists determinately [in the divine] essence, however, it is for the divine intellect a basis for understanding that truth — and this naturally, insofar as [this understanding] is based upon the [divine] essence. [The divine intellect] understands all necessary principles naturally, as if before the act of the divine will (since their truth does not depend upon that act and they would be understood even if, *per impossibile*, [the divine will] were not willing). Thus, the divine essence is the basis for [the divine intellect's] cognizing these things at that prior [instant], since they are true then. Not, indeed, that those truths move the divine intellect, nor [are] their terms even [required] for the apprehending of such truth. But the divine essence is the basis for cognizing such complexes as well as simples.

But then [at that prior instant those complexes] are not true contingents, since there is nothing in virtue of which they have determinate truth then. Once the determination of the divine will has been posited, however, they are already true, and at that second instant the [divine] essence will be the basis for cognizing them.

The following sort of example is offered. Suppose that one act, always actualized (*semper stans*) in my visual capacity, is the basis for [my] seeing an object, and that, as a result of another [act of] presenting, now this color is present, now that. [In that case] my eye will see now this, now that, but by means of one and the same [act of] vision. The only difference will be in the priority of seeing, because of an object's having been presented earlier or later; and if one color were present naturally and another freely, there would be no formal* difference in my vision. For its part, indeed, the eye would see both naturally and yet would see one contingently and the other necessarily, insofar as the one is present contingently and the other necessarily. If it is posited* that the divine intellect cognizes the existence of things in both those ways, it is clear that in both ways there is a determination of the divine intellect with respect to the existent thing in relation to which the divine will is determined. And [there is] the certainty of infallibility, since the will cannot be determined without the intellect determinately ap-

[8]E.g., a conjunction of the simples whiteness and largeness at t_1 for a toadstool just sprouting now, at t_0. See Appendix II, p. 99.

prehending that which the will determines. And [the divine intellect cognizes] immutably, since the intellect and the will are immutable. And the contingency of the cognized object is consistent with these [claims], since the will, willing something determinately, wills it contingently.

E One can argue against this view*[9]: first, against the claim that a nonevident capacity for opposites — i.e., for opposites without succession — accompanies the first freedom, for this does not seem true. The reason is that a capacity that can be actualized by no capacity, not even by an infinite [capacity], is not to be posited. But this nonevident capacity can be actualized by no capacity, since if it were actualized the will would will something at t_1 and not will it at t_1, and so contradictories would evidently be true at one and the same time.

Suppose it is said that if it is actualized, 'the will willed X at t_1' is no longer true, nor even 'the will wills X at t_1,' since from the very fact that the will does not will X at t_1 it follows that 'the will wills X at t_1' is not true.

On the contrary, it is generally conceded by philosophers and theologians that God cannot make what is past not to be past without its afterwards always being true to say that it was past. Therefore, since by hypothesis 'the will wills X at t_1' is now determinately true and consequently ['the will willed X at t_1'] will always be true afterwards and 'the will does not* will X at t_1' never was true, after t_1 'the will did not* will X at t_1' always was impossible. Furthermore, now afterwards it is true to say that 'the will does not will X at t_1' could not have been true at the instant at which its opposite was true, even though it was true earlier, since frequently a true proposition becomes impossible.[10]

F Suppose it is said that that [nonevident] capacity could be actualized, since [the will] can cease to will X at t_1.

[9]Boehner supplies the subtitle "Against Scotus's View" for the text from marginal letter **F** to marginal letter **L**.

[10]The view that a proposition that is true at one time may (and frequently does) become impossible is out of keeping with Ockham's treatment of modalities generally and seems specifically out of place here. In all likelihood '*possibilis*' should be read for '*vera*' in these last two clauses, in which case the translation would read "even though it was possible earlier, since frequently a possible proposition becomes impossible."

I answer that this does not hold good, since *this* capacity for opposites is evident and with succession. For at one instant 'the will wills X at t_1' will be true, and at another instant 'the will does not will X at t_1' will be true.[11] But that both are true at the same instant as a result of any capacity whatever is absolutely impossible. In the same way it is impossible that 'a created will wills X at t_1' is true at first and that 'a [created] will never willed X at t_1' is true afterwards. And so with respect to creatures it is universally true that there never is a capacity for opposite objects without succession any more than for opposite acts. Indeed, by one and the same argument it can be "proved" that there is a capacity of a created will for opposite acts without succession and for opposite objects. But his argument does not come to a successful conclusion, and yet[12] it must be conceded that the will when it causes causes contingently.

But there can be two causes of this truth. It is said to cause contingently either (*a*) because it is possible that at one and the same instant it is true to say that [the will] does not cause (and this is impossible, because having posited that it is causing at some instant it is impossible that it is not causing at that same instant), or (*b*) because it can cease from the act at another instant, freely, without any variation occurring in itself or another, and not as a result of the cessation of another cause, so that at *another* instant it is not causing, not that at that *same* instant it is not causing. And the will does cause contingently in that way.

[Causing] in that way it is not a natural cause, however, for a cause acting naturally always acts, unless it is changed or something new happens to it, either because some cause ceases to cause or in some other way. Even if none of these is the case (*sine quo omni*), the will can cease from the act in virtue of its freedom alone.

G   As to the form of the argument, I maintain that at the instant at which [the will] causes it causes contingently and not necessarily. But it does not follow from this that this capacity of a cause for the opposite [of what it causes] is [a capacity] for its opposite without succession. For it is impossible that [such a capacity] should be actualized by any capacity whatever. But there is a capacity for its opposite, a capacity that can be actualized in succession. For I

[11]See *Treatise*, n. 111.
[12]Reading '*tamen*' for '*quia*.'

take [as an example] heat heating wood. That heat can *not* heat, and this capacity [for not heating] can be actualized by the destruction of the agent of the heat, or by the removal of the patient, or by the interposition of an impediment, or by the withdrawal of a coacting cause (suppose that God does not will to coact with it), or by the full actualization (*perfectionem*) of the end product (since fully actualized heat is produced in such a way that a more fully actualized [heat] cannot be produced by that same heat). Besides these ways [in which a natural cause can cease from causing an act], there is one additional way in which a created will can cease from causing an act — viz., all by itself — even though none of the afore-mentioned things is lacking but all are posited, and this and nothing else is the will causing contingently.

H   From this it is clear that it is inconsistent to say that the divine will as naturally prior posits its effect in reality at t_1 in such a way that it can *not* posit it in reality at the same instant. For there are no such instants of nature as he [Scotus] imagines, nor is there in the first instant of nature such an indifference as regards positing and not positing. Rather, if at some instant it posits its effect in reality, it is impossible by means of any capacity whatever that both the instant occurs and [the effect] does not occur at that instant, just as it is impossible by means of any capacity whatever that contradictories are true at one and the same time.

I maintain, therefore, that in general there is never a capacity by means of which opposites are verified without succession. Indeed, it is impossible that God should have an object in view and not have it in view, unless either there is at least some succession in actuality or it coexists (and in that case there would be a change in everything else).[13]

J   [One can argue,] moreover, against what he says about the determination of the divine will: first, that the principal conclusion is not true. For when something is determined contingently, so that it is possible that it never was determined, one cannot have certain and infallible evidence as a result of such a determination. But the

[13]The second of these alternatives is not clearly expressed. From everything else Ockham has to say on this point, however, it seems fairly obvious that in his view the only real alternative is the first one, and that he here introduces the notion of God's having an object in view and not having it in view without succession only in order to point up its absurdity.

divine will is determined in such a way that it is still possible that it never was determined. Therefore one cannot have certain and infallible evidence as a result of such a determination, as a consequence of which (*ex quo*) it can simply never have been.[14] And so it seems that the determination of the divine will, if it occurred, would produce too little.

Moreover, however much the certainty of [God's] knowledge can be preserved by the determination of the [divine] will in respect of all effects produced by the will, and even in respect of all effects of natural causes with which the divine will coacts, still it does not seem that the certainty of [God's knowledge in respect of] future acts of a created will itself can be preserved by that determination. For if the divine will is determined in respect of all things I ask whether or not the determination or production of a created will necessarily follows that determination. If so, then a created will acts naturally just as does any natural cause. For when the divine will exists as determined to one of [two] opposites it is not in the power of any natural cause not to coact, and also when it is not determined a natural cause does not coact. In the same way when the divine will exists as determined a created will would coact, nor would it have it in its power not to coact, and consequently no act of a created will would be imputable to [that will] itself. If, however, the determination of a created will does not necessarily follow the determination of the divine will, then the determination of the divine will does not suffice for knowing whether an effect will be posited, but the determination of a created will is required, which is not yet or [at any rate] was not from eternity. Therefore God did not from eternity have certain cognition of future contingents as a result of the determination of the divine will.

Moreover, however much a created will is determined to one or the other part [of a contradiction] and however much the [divine] intellect sees that determination, nevertheless since our will can cease from that determination and not be determined, the [divine] intellect does not have certain cognition of that part. Therefore seeing the determination of a [created] will, a will that can *not* be determined to that part, does not suffice for certain cognition of that part.

[14]Ockham is referring here to the "consequent" rather than the "antecedent" will of God. See Introduction, pp. 17–20.

K   Moreover, his claim that at the first instant the divine intellect presents simples [to itself], and that the divine will afterwards chooses one part, and that the intellect thereafter has evident cognition of that part, does not seem to be true. For there is no process or priority or contradiction in God such that the divine intellect at one instant does not have evident cognition of future contingents and at another instant does have [such cognition of them]. For to say that the divine intellect receives any perfection from something else would be to posit an imperfection [in the divine intellect].

L   Therefore as regards the question[15] I say that it is to be held indubitably that God knows all future contingents certainly and evidently. But to explain this clearly and to describe the way in which He knows all future contingents is impossible for any intellect in this [present] condition.

M   And I maintain that the Philosopher would say that God does not know some future contingents evidently and certainly, and for the following reason. What is not true in itself cannot be known at a time at which it is not true in itself. But a future contingent absolutely dependent on a free capacity is not true in itself, since no reason can be given in accord with [that description of] it why the one part is true rather than the other. And so either both parts are true or neither [is true], and it is not possible that both parts are true; therefore neither is true. Consequently neither is known.

This argument does not come to a successful conclusion, according to the Philosopher's way [of thinking], except as regards those [future contingents] that are in the power of a will. But it does not hold good in connection with those that are not in the power of a will but depend absolutely on natural causes — e.g., that the sun will rise, and thus also as regards others [of that sort]. This is because a natural cause is determined for one part [of a contradiction], and no natural causes can be impeded except by a free cause. Nevertheless, they can be impeded by it in respect of one determined effect though not in respect of any and every [effect].[16]

This argument notwithstanding, it must nevertheless be maintained that God has evident cognition of all future contingents. But

[15]Boehner supplies the subtitle "Ockham's Own View" for the text from marginal letter **L** to marginal letter **P**.

[16]Cf. Appendix II, p. 106.

I do not know how to describe the way [in which He has it]. Still, it can be said that God Himself, or the divine essence, is a single intuitive cognition as much of Himself as of all things creatable and uncreatable — [a cognition] so perfect and so clear that it is also evident cognition of all things past, future, and present. Thus just as our intellect can have evident cognition of some contingent propositions from our intuitive intellective cognition of the extremes [of those propositions],[17] so the divine essence itself is a cognition (*cognitio et notitia*) by which is known not only what is true (both necessary and contingent) regarding the present but also which part of a contradiction [involving future contingents] will be true and which will be false. And perhaps this is not as a result of the determination of His will. But even if it is supposed, *per impossibile*, that the divine cognition, existing as perfect as it now is, is neither the total nor the partial efficient cause of contingent effects, there would still be the cognition by which it would be evidently known by God which part of a contradiction will be true and which will be false. And this would not be because future contingents would be present to Him to be cognized either by means of ideas or by means of reasons, but by the divine essence itself or the divine cognition, which is the cognition by which it is known what is false and what is true, what was false and what was true, what will be false and what will be true.

This conclusion, although it cannot be proved *a priori* by means of the natural reason available to us, nevertheless can be proved by means of the authorities of the Bible and the Saints, which are sufficiently well known. But I pass over those things at present.

N   In the view of certain scholars (*artistis*), however, it must be known that although God knows regarding all future contingents which part will be true and which false, still 'God knows that this part will be true' is not necessary. Indeed, it is contingent to such an extent that although 'God knows that this part of the contradiction will be true' is true, it is still possible that it will never have been true. And in that case there is a capacity for its opposite without any succession, since it is possible that it will never have been. But it is different in the case of a created will, since after a created will

---

[17] Cf. Introduction, pp. 25–26.

will have performed some act it is not possible that it is afterwards true to say that it never performed such an act.

Regarding *de possibili* propositions I maintain, as do others, that the proposition 'it is possible that God willing that *A* will be wills that it will not be' and others like it must be distinguished with respect to composition and division. In the sense of composition it is indicated that this is possible: 'God willing that *A* will be does not will that *A* will be,' and this is impossible, since it includes a contradiction. In the sense of division it is indicated that God willing that *A* will be can *not* will that *A* will be, and that is true.

And suppose one says "suppose that it is posited in reality (and it is not impossible that that should happen); as a consequence 'God wills that *A* will be' and 'God does not will that *A* will be' hold good at one and the same time." In that case I maintain that when that possible [proposition] has been posited in reality an impossible [proposition] does not follow. But it must not be posited in reality in this way: 'God willing that *A* will be does not will that *A* will be.' Rather, it must be posited in reality in this way: 'God does not will that *A* will be.' And when that has been posited in reality nothing impossible follows, for only this follows: 'God never willed that *A* will be.' And that is not impossible but contingent, just as its contradictory — 'God wills that *A* will be' — always was contingent.

O ⋅   On the basis of the preceding remarks one can respond to the question [as follows]. God has determinate knowledge of future contingents because He knows determinately which part of a contradiction will be true and which false. But that He has [necessary] knowledge of future contingents can be understood in two ways; either that the knowledge by which future contingents are known is necessary, or that that knowledge is known necessarily. I maintain that God has necessary knowledge of future contingents in the first way, for there is one single cognition in God that is a cognition of complexes and of non-complexes, of necessaries and of contingents, and universally of all things imaginable. And that knowledge is the divine essence itself, which is necessary and immutable. That God has necessary knowledge of future contingents is understood in the second way as follows: that God necessarily knows this future contingent. It is not to be granted that He has necessary knowledge in that way, for just as it contingently will be, so God contingently knows that it will be.

P   In response to the first principal [argument][18] it can be said
that one or the other part of the contradiction is determinately
true, so that it is not false but is contingently true. Therefore it is
true in such a way that it can be false and can never have been true.

And suppose one says that a proposition true at some time of
the present has [corresponding to it] a necessary proposition about
the past — e.g., if 'Socrates is seated' is true at some time, 'Socrates
was seated' will be necessary ever afterwards; therefore if '*A* is true'
is true now (*A* being such a contingent proposition), '*A* was true'
will always be true and necessary. In that case it must be said that
when such a proposition about the present is equivalent to a proposition about the future or depends on the truth of a future
[proposition], it is not required that a necessary proposition about
the past correspond to the true proposition about the present. And
this is the case in the matter under discussion.

In response to the second [principal argument] it is clear that
'God has necessary knowledge of *A*' does not follow unless 'has
necessary knowledge' is taken in the second way. Therefore God
necessarily knows *A*. But when 'has necessary knowledge' is taken
in the first way the consequence does not hold good.

The response to the argument in opposition is clear from the
preceding remarks.

Distinction 39

A   Regarding the thirty-ninth distinction I ask whether God
could know more than He knows.

It seems that He could, for He can know something that He
does not know; therefore He can know more than He knows. The
antecedent is clear, for He does not now know that I am in Rome,
and He can know that since[19] it can be true.

On the contrary, God's knowledge can neither increase nor
decrease; therefore He cannot know more than He knows.

B   As to the question, it must first be seen how the question is
to be understood. And it must be known that it is one thing to ask
whether God can know more than He knows and another to ask
whether God can know something that He does not know.

---

[18]Boehner supplies the subtitle "In Response to the Principal Arguments" for
the text from marginal letter **P** to the end of Distinction 38.

[19]Reading '*quia*' for '*igitur*.'

In the second place it must be known that 'know' (*scire*) is taken here in two ways — broadly and strictly. In the first way it is the same as 'cognize' (*cognoscere*) insofar as cognizing is common to all things. And in this way God knows — i.e., cognizes — all things: complex and non-complex, necessary and contingent, true, false, and impossible. In the strict sense 'know' is the same as 'cognize what is true'; and in that sense nothing is known but what is true.

C   On this basis I maintain as regards the question that if 'know' is taken in the broad sense God cannot know more [than He knows] or know something that He does not know, for He cannot acquire the knowledge of anything for the first time (*de novo*).

If 'know' is taken in the second way I maintain that God cannot know more than He knows. The reason for this is that everything true is known by God, and the number of truths is always the same (*et semper aequalia sunt vera*). Thus it is not possible that more things are true at one time than at another, since at each time one or the other part of a contradiction is true, and nothing is true but what is one or the other part of a contradiction. And it is not possible that both parts of a contradiction are true, and so there are always as many true things at one time as at another, and neither more nor less, although some things are true at one time that are not true at another time. And in general, if something becomes false that was true earlier, something will become true that was false earlier.

Despite the fact that God can[not] know more than He knows, God can know something that He does not know, if 'know' is taken in the second way. Just as something can be true that was not true earlier, so something can be known by God that was not known earlier. For everything true, when it is true, is known by God; and when it is not true, it is not known by God. For example, it is not now known by God that I am in Rome, because it is not now true. Nevertheless, it can be known by God, because it can be true; and if it will be true, it will be known by God.

And suppose it is said that in that case God could change from knowing to not knowing and vice versa, which is impossible. This can be confirmed, since although something can be denominated for the first time by a relative denomination or a relative or connotative denominable without a change in it, nevertheless it cannot be denominated for the first time by an absolute denominable without a change in it.[20] But knowledge is an absolute perfection in God. Therefore God cannot for the first time come to know (*fieri sciens*) this knowable without changing.

Further, it is the same thing to know that Socrates is seated and afterwards to know that Socrates was seated. Therefore on this basis when God first knows 'Socrates is seated' and afterwards knows 'Socrates was seated' He does not know something else, but the same thing.

In response to the first of these [arguments], I maintain that although God first does not know this and afterwards does know it, it does not follow that God changes; for in order to verify such contradictories of God [successively], a mere change in a creature suffices. In the same way a mere change in a creature suffices [to bring it about] that He is first not creating and afterwards creating.

As to the confirmation, I maintain that knowledge, as we are now speaking of knowledge, is not strictly speaking an absolute denominable but a connotative denominable, since 'know' connotes that that which is known is true and not false. And since one and the same thing can be first false and afterwards true, therefore without any change on God's part something can be first not known by God and be afterwards known [by Him].

In response to the second [argument], I maintain that it is not the same thing to know that Socrates is seated and to know that Socrates was seated unless 'know' is taken for that cognition which is God's own (*a parte Dei*). Nevertheless 'God knows that Socrates is seated' and 'God knows that Socrates was seated' are neither the same nor equipollent nor interchangeable, since the one can be true while the other is (*existente*) false. And if there were two [men],

---

[20]On denomination or denominative predication see *Treatise*, n. 6. See also Matthew C. Menges, *The Concept of Univocity Regarding the Predication of God and Creature According to William Ockham* (Franciscan Institute Publications, Philosophy Series, No. 9; St. Bonaventure, N.Y., The Franciscan Institute, 1952), pp. 47–51. The word 'denominable' (*denominabile*) occurs misleadingly here in a context in which Ockham ordinarily uses 'denominative' (*denominativum*). As an example of a relative denominative take 'shorter than Theaetetus.' While the boy Theaetetus is growing up, the man Socrates is first taller than Theaetetus, then the same height as Theaetetus, and finally shorter than Theaetetus. But when Socrates is for the first time correctly denominated by the relative denominative 'shorter than Theaetetus' it is not as a consequence of any change having taken place in Socrates. On the other hand, when Socrates is for the first time correctly denominated by the absolute denominative 'blind' it is as a consequence of a change having taken place in him.

one of whom believed that Socrates was seated and the other that Socrates had been seated, it would be possible that at one and the same time the one was mistaken and the other was not mistaken.

And if one says that it would follow from this that God would know stateables (*enuntiabilia*) and consequently would be compounding and dividing,[21] which is absurd (*inconveniens*), then it must be said that God cognizes all stateables without any composition and division, for He cognizes all things in one absolutely simple cognition.

In response to the principal argument it is clear that God can know something that He did not know earlier. But this is not because He was earlier ignorant of something knowable or true, but because something is now true that was not true earlier but was false earlier.

In response to the argument in opposition, it is clear that God's knowledge can neither increase nor decrease. Nevertheless, He can know something that He did not know earlier. In the same way God's power can neither increase nor decrease, and nevertheless He can produce something that He did not produce earlier.

---

[21]Ockham evidently uses the noun 'stateable' (*enuntiabile*) as did such thirteenth-century logicians as William of Sherwood and Peter of Spain, to designate that which is expressed in a statement (*enuntiatio*) or proposition. (See Norman Kretzmann, *William of Sherwood's Treatise on Syncategorematic Words* [Minneapolis, University of Minnesota Press, 1968], Chapter 14, n. 10.) In this passage "compounding and dividing" is the compounding and dividing of the subject and predicate terms of stateables with or from one another — i.e., the producing of affirmative and negative stateables — an activity that cannot be consistently ascribed to an omniscient, immutable being.

APPENDIX II

Commentary on Aristotle's *De interpretatione,* Chapter 9[22]

[*Therefore as regards the things that are and that have happened, it is necessary that either the affirmation or the negation be true (or false). Indeed, as regards universals [expressed] universally, [it is] always [necessary] that the one is true but the other false; also as regards those that are singulars, as has been said. But as regards universals that are not expressed universally, it is not necessary; these, however, have also been spoken of.*] (18a28–18a32)

As regards those that are singular and future, however, it is not like that. For if every affirmation and negation is either true or false, it is necessary that everything either is or is not. Thus if this person says that something is going to be, but that one says that that same thing is not going to be, it is evident that it is necessary that one or the other of them is saying what is true (if every affirmation is either true or false). For both will not be the case together in such circumstances. For if it is true to say that a thing is white or is not white, it is necessary that it is white or is not white. And if it is white or is not white, it is true to affirm or to deny this. And if it is not [white], he says what is false; and if he says what is false, it is not [white]. That is why it is necessary that either the affirmation or the negation is true (or false). Nothing, there-

[22]Before each portion of Ockham's commentary the Aristotelian passage on which he is specifically commenting is quoted in its entirety. In the translation these passages (indented and italicized) have been translated not from Aristotle's Greek but from medieval Latin versions. (We used mainly the version printed in the *Expositio aurea,* an edition of Ockham's commentaries on Aristotle's logical works [and the *Tractatus de praedestinatione et de praescientia Dei et de futuris contingentibus*] published at Bologna in 1496, comparing it with and occasionally adjusting it to the generally preferable version to be found in the *Aristotelis opera* of Venice, 1562. Definitive editions of Boethius's and William of Moerbeke's Latin translations have been published as Volume II, 1–2, of *Aristoteles Latinus,* ed. L. Minio-Paluello; Bruges-Paris: Desclee de Brouwer, 1965.) It will often be instructive to compare these passages with the corresponding passages in J. L. Ackrill's translation from the Greek (*Aristotle's Categories and De Interpretatione,* Oxford, The Clarendon Press, 1963). The first paragraph of the Aristotle text, here enclosed in brackets, usually occurs as the first paragraph of Chapter 9. In Ockham's commentary, however, it is treated as the last paragraph of the preceding chapter and forms no part of the basis of his examination of Aristotle's treatment of future contingents.

fore, either is or happens, or will be or will not be, by chance or fortuitously — but all things of necessity and not fortuitously — since either the one who says it or the one who denies it is correct. For it would equally well (similiter) *happen or not happen, since what is fortuitous is no more thus than not thus, nor will it be.* (18a33-18b8)

In this part [Chapter 9] the Philosopher determines the way in which opposed singular* propositions about the future are related to truth and falsity.

It is divided into two parts [9.1 and 9.2].[23] For he first shows that in some [propositions] about the future there is no determinate truth [18a33-19a22]. In the second place he shows how they are related to truth and falsity [19a23-19b4].

The first part [9.1] is divided into three parts [9.11, 9.12, 9.13]. For he first shows that if truth were determinate in all [propositions] about the future all things would come about of necessity [18a33-18b25]. In the second place he infers several absurdities from that absurdity [18b26-19a6]. In the third place he shows that this would be impossible [19a7-19a22].

The first part [9.11] is divided into two parts [9.111 and 9.112]. For he first shows that this absurdity follows [18a33-18b16]. In the

---

[23]Ockham organizes his commentary by subdividing Aristotle's chapter into several parts. He identifies some of these parts in his commentary by inserting the opening words of the appropriate Aristotelian passage into his text. We have omitted those identifying passages from our translation and have supplied a system of numerical designations to aid the reader in following Ockham's analysis of Aristotle's chapter. The numerical designations derive from the following organizational scheme; the figures in brackets designate the corresponding passages in *De interpretatione*, Chapter 9.

9.1 [18a33-19a22]
  9.11 [18a33-18b25]
    9.111 [18a33-18b16]
      9.1111[18a33-18b8]
      9.1112 [18b9-18b16]
    9.112 [18b17-18b25]
      9.1121 [18b17-18b20]
      9.1122 [18b20-18b25]
  9.12 [18b26-19a6]
  9.13 [19a7-19a22]
9.2 [19a23-19b4]
  9.21 [19a23-19a32]
  9.22 [19a32-19b4]
    9.221 [19a32-19a39]
    9.222 [19a39-19b4]

second place he incidentally shows that not both parts of such a contradiction are false [18b17–18b25].

The first part [9.111] is divided into two parts [9.1111 and 9.1112] in view of the fact that he proves its conclusion by means of two arguments [18a33–18b8 and 18b9–18b16].[24]

In the first part [9.1111] he puts forward [the first of] the two arguments, setting out the conclusion first, saying that as regards singular [propositions] about the future it is not as it is regarding those about the past and about the present, in that it is not always the case that one part of a contradiction [involving singular propositions about the future] is true and the other false as it is regarding those about the past and about the present. And he proves this by arguing to an impossibility as follows. If every affirmative and [every] negative proposition is either determinately true or determinately false, then if one says 'this will be' and another says 'this will not be,' one of them must be saying what is determinately true (if any and every proposition is either determinately true or determinately false). For example, if someone says 'this will be white' and another says 'this will not be white,' it must be that one is saying what is determinately true and the other is speaking determinately falsely (*determinate mentiatur*). But this is false, since in that case nothing would happen by chance or fortuitously (*ad utrumlibet*), but all things would happen of necessity. This last consequence is clear, since what happens fortuitously is no more determined to one part that to the other—i.e., no more determined to being than to not being. Therefore if it is determined that this will be or that it will not be, it happens not fortuitously but of necessity.

Furthermore, if it is white now, it was true to say earlier that it would be white. For that reason it was always true to say of any of the things that have happened that it would be. But if it was always true to say that it is or will be, the thing in question cannot not be or not be going to be. But if something cannot not happen, it is impossible that it not happen; and if it is impossible that something not happen, it is necessary that it happen. Regarding all things that are going to be, therefore, it is necessary that they happen. Thus nothing will be fortuitous or by chance; for if it is by chance, it is not of necessity. (18b9–18b16)

Here [in part 9.1112] he puts forward the second argument—

[24]This short paragraph is omitted from Boehner's edition. Among the sources of the edition only E, the Bologna printed edition of 1496, includes it.

viz., that if this is now white and if truth is determinate in [propositions] about the future, then 'this will be white' was true earlier. Indeed, 'this will be white' was always true. But if it was always going to be, then it could not not be going to be. Therefore it could not not happen; therefore it was impossible that it not happen; therefore it was necessary that it happen (and so on with regard to other [singular propositions about the future]). And consequently all things happen of necessity, and nothing happens by chance or fortuitously.

This argument is based on the proposition that a singular proposition true about the past is necessary. Therefore if 'this is white' is true now, "'this will be white' was true" is necessary. Consequently, it is necessary that it happen, and it cannot come about otherwise.

Nor, however, can it be said that neither is true, so that it neither will be nor will not be. For, in the first place, when the affirmation is false the negation will not be true; and when the negation is false, it turns out that the affirmation is not true. (18b17–18b20)

Here [in part 9.1121] he incidentally shows that not both parts of such a contradiction are false, as some might sophistically claim (*cavillare*), and [he shows this] by means of two arguments. The first argument is that whenever an affirmation is false the negation opposed to it will be true. Similarly, when a negation is false the affirmation opposed to it will be true. Therefore if 'this will be' is false, 'this will not be' will be true; and if 'this will not be' is false, 'this will be' will be true. Consequently if the former two are false, the latter two will be true [which is absurd].

Moreover, if it is true to say [of something] that it is white and large, it must be both. But if it will be tomorrow, it must be tomorrow. If, however, it neither will be nor will not be tomorrow, it will not be fortuitous. For example, a sea-battle: for it must be that the sea-battle neither happens nor does not happen. (18b20–18b25)

[In part 9.1122] he puts forward the second argument, which is that if it is true to say of something that it is white and large, both have to be verified of one and the same thing at one and the same time. Therefore, similarly, if it is true to say determinately that this will be white and large tomorrow, tomorrow it will be true to say that this is white and large. Therefore, in the same way, if it is now true to say determinately that it neither will be nor will not be—say, that a sea-battle neither will be nor will not be—that would have to be the case: viz., that a sea-battle neither will be nor will not be*—if both parts [of the contradiction] are false.

For if 'there will be a sea-battle' is false, it will be true to say determinately that there will not be a sea-battle; and if 'there will not be a sea-battle' is false, it will be true to say that there will be a sea-battle. Consequently it will be true to say 'there neither is nor is not a sea-battle,' which is impossible. Therefore it is impossible that 'there will be a sea-battle tomorrow' and 'there will not be a sea-battle tomorrow' are both determinately false.

It must be known in this connection that as regards singular propositions about the future in which the subject is a detached demonstrative pronoun or a simple proper name of some one single thing, this rule is true—viz., that if it will be such, then it will be true to say that it is such. And a corresponding rule holds as regards [singular] propositions about the past. But if the subject is a common term or one composed of a common term and a demonstrative pronoun, the rule is not universally true—neither as regards propositions about the past nor as regards propositions about the future. For 'what is true will be false' is true now, and nevertheless 'what is true is false' will never be true. Similarly, 'this truth, that you are seated, will be false' is true; nevertheless 'this truth is false' will never be true. Similarly, 'what is white was black' is true now; nevertheless 'what is white is black' was never true. Similarly, 'this white man was black' is true; nevertheless 'this white man is black' was never true. But if a proposition such as 'this was white' is true now, then at some time 'this is white' was true. And if 'this will be false' is true now, then 'this is false' will be true. And so on with regard to others [of this sort].

And it must be understood that the corresponding rule is to be understood in a corresponding way as regards all modal propositions taken in the sense of division or equivalent to [one taken in] the sense of division. Thus "this can be white; therefore 'this is white' is possible" follows correctly. Nevertheless "what is black can be white; therefore 'what is black is white' is possible" does not follow. And so on with regard to other [such inferences].

These absurdities, therefore, and others like them are those that occur if it is necessary of every affirmation and negation, either as regards universals expressed universally or as regards those that are singulars, that this one of the opposites is true but that one false. Nothing, however, is fortuitous — neither as regards things that are nor as regards things that are happening — but all things happen of necessity. Thus there will be no need to deliberate or to take trouble, [thinking] that if we do this, this will be, but if not, this will not be. For nothing prevents someone's saying a thousand years ago that this was going to be and another's saying that it was not going to be. Thus whichever of them it was true to say then will be of necessity. Nor does it make any difference if anyone will have said the negation or will not have said it. For it is evident that the real things are thus even if one person will not have affirmed it or another denied it. For it is not because of the affirming or the denying that it will be or will not be, nor [is it a question of] a thousand years ago rather than at any other time. Thus if at every time things were such that one or the other would be said truly, it was necessary that this happen; and for every one of the things that happen the circumstances were always such that it would happen of necessity. For what anyone truly says will be cannot not happen; and of what has happened it was always true to say that it would be. (18b26–19a6)

In this part [9.12] the Philosopher infers several absurdities from the absurdity already deduced, saying that these absurdities and others like them are those that follow if it is granted, both as regards universal [propositions] and as regards singular [propositions], that it is necessary that one part of a contradiction be true and the other part false. For in that case nothing would happen fortuitously, but all things would happen of necessity. From this it follows further that there would be no need to deliberate or to take trouble, since from the fact that it is determined [it follows that] it will happen as it was determined from the outset, whether or not we deliberate.

Nor does it hold good to say that it is not true to say that this will be except as regards the immediate rather than the distant future, for it makes no difference whether it is true now or a thousand years ago.

Nor does it hold good to say that one or the other of those who say either 'this will be' or 'this will not be' says what is false *because of the fact that he says it.* For an expression (*oratio*) is not true or false because of someone's affirming or denying it but because the state of affairs is in reality as it is signified [in the expression] or is not as it is signified.

And so it makes no difference to say that 'this will be' is true either a thousand years ago or more recently (*post*); thus if it is determinately true that this will be or [that this] will not be, all things will happen of necessity and nothing will happen by chance or fortuitously.

What if these things are not possible? For we see that there is a source of things that will be, both because we deliberate and because we act in some way; and that as regards things that are not always in actuality it is altogether possible to be and likewise not to be. As regards these things, both being and not being occur, and therefore both happening and not happening. And many other such things are evident to us. For example, it is possible that this cloak be cut up, and [yet] it is not cut up but wears out first. It is likewise possible, however, that it not be cut up, for it would not first wear out if it were not possible that it not be cut up. Therefore [the same is true] also as regards other things that are going to be that are spoken of in terms of this potentiality. It is evident, therefore, that not all things either are or happen of necessity. But some indeed are fortuitous, and the affirmation is no more true than the negation. In others, however, it is one or the other in many instances; nevertheless the one [that does not happen in many instances] can happen, even though very seldom. (19a7–19a22)

Here [in part 9.13] he shows that not all things come about of necessity, saying that if these things that have been deduced are impossible — viz., that there is no need to deliberate or to take trouble, and that all things are of necessity — then it is evident that the position he considers as regards future contingents is impossible — viz., that one part of a contradiction [involving them] is true and the other false.

He proves that it is impossible that all things come about of necessity in the following way. Those things of which we are the sources (*principia*) and regarding which we deliberate and that are not always actual are possible, both to be and not to be, or do not come about of necessity. But there are many future things of which we are the sources and regarding which we deliberate. Therefore there are many such things that do not come about of necessity.

He shows this also by means of an example. For it is possible that a cloak be cut up, and nevertheless that cloak is *not* cut up but wears out and is destroyed by becoming old. Similarly, it is possible that the cloak not be cut up, and nevertheless that cloak *is* cut up afterwards. From these considerations, he concludes that it is evident regarding many future things that they do not come about of necessity, but some come about fortuitously and others [by chance] as [they do] in many instances.

Therefore it is necessary that what is is when it is, and that what is not is not when it is not. But it is not necessary that everything that is is, nor is it necessary that everything that is not is not. For that everything that is is necessarily when it is is not the same as that it simply is of necessity. Similarly as regards what is not. And the same account applies as regards contradiction: that it is necessary that everything either is or is not, and is going to be or is not going to be. Nevertheless it is not for one who divides [the contradiction into its two parts] to say that one or the other is necessary. I say, however, that it is necessary that there is going to be or is not going to be a sea-battle tomorrow; not, however, that it is necessary that there is going to be a sea-battle tomorrow, or that there is not going to be one — though it is necessary that it is going to be or is not going to be. (19a23–19a32)

In this part [9.2] he shows how opposed propositions about the future are related to truth and falsity — he does that [9.21] in the first place [19a23–19a32]. In the second place [9.22] he infers two corollaries [19a32–19b4]. In the first part [9.221] he shows how the parts of a contradiction are related to truth and falsity [19a32–19a39]. In the second part [9.222] he shows that in [contradictions involving] future contingents neither part is determinately true [19a39–19b4].

First, therefore, [in part 9.21] he intends [to prove] this conclusion, that necessity is predicated of the whole disjunctive proposition composed of both parts of a contradiction — and this whether [it is a contradiction] involving propositions about the present or about the past or [a contradiction] involving propositions about the future. Thus [as regards propositions about the future] just as regards propositions about the present or about the past, he says that for everything that is, when it is it is necessary that it is; and for everything that is not, when it is not it is necessary that it is not.* (For it is not the same to say 'for everything that is, when it is it is necessary that it is' and 'for everything that is, it is necessary that it is.') Thus in a contradiction it is necessary that it either is or is not — i.e., the disjunctive proposition composed of both parts of a contradiction about the present is necessary. Similarly, that it either is going to be or is not going to be — i.e., the disjunctive proposition composed of the two parts of a contradiction about the future is necessary. But* it is not necessary taken separately — i.e., neither part of the disjunctive is necessary. For example, the disjunctive 'either there will be a sea-battle tomorrow or there will not be a sea-battle tomorrow' is necessary, and yet neither 'there will be a sea-battle tomorrow' nor 'there will not be a sea-battle tomorrow' is necessary, despite the fact that the disjunctive is necessary.

It must be known that the proposition 'for everything that is, when it is it is necessary that it is' is simply false taken literally (*de virtute sermonis*). This is because it can be taken literally only if it is taken to be temporal or to have a temporal subject.

If it is temporal it amounts to this: 'for everything that is, it is necessary that it is when it is.' And this is false, for the truth of a temporal proposition requires the truth of both parts for one and the same time. But the first part — 'for everything that is, it is necessary that it is' — is simply false; therefore the whole temporal proposition is false.

If it has a temporal subject it is also false, for in that case it denotes that all that of which this whole predicate[25] 'is when it is' is verified is necessary. And this is false, for this whole is verified of any and every existing thing, and yet it is not the case that for any and every existing thing it is necessary that it is.

But in the sense in which he intended the proposition it is true, for by it he meant this: 'for each thing (*de omni illo*) that is, it is necessarily verified that it is if it is that time [at which it is].' That is, [he meant] that this consequence is necessary even though it is not formal: 'it is this time; therefore that [thing] is.' For example, if Socrates is at t_1 (*in A tamquam in aliquo tempore*) the consequence 'it is t_1; therefore Socrates is' always is necessary. Similarly, by 'for everything that is, when it is it is necessary that it is' he means that it will always be true to say that this was at the time at which it was. (It suffices [to present] the Philosopher's point of view. It could be explained, but I pass over that for the sake of brevity.) And that is not the case with 'for everything that is, it is necessary that it is,' for 'there is time; therefore A is' (where A is something that is) does not follow, as 'it is this time; therefore A is' (where A is something that is at this time) does follow.

Therefore, since expressions are true according to the way in which the real things are, it is evident that as regards any that are such that they and their contraries occur fortuitously, it is necessary that their contradiction likewise be such. This occurs in those that are not always or that are not always not. For it is necessary that one or the

[25]Reading '*praedicatum*' for '*subiectum*.'

other part of their contradiction is true (or false) — not, however, this one or that one,
but fortuitously; and not that the one is true rather than the other, yet not already
true (or false). (19a32–19a39)

Here [in part 9.221] he shows that neither part of a contradiction involving propositions about the future is determinately true. He does this in the following way. Expressions are true according to the way in which the real things that are indicated by the expressions are. But the thing that is indicated by a future contingent [proposition], on the basis of which it is fortuitous, is no more determined to be going to be than to be going not to be. Therefore the proposition indicating it is no more true than false. Nevertheless, the Philosopher adds that although it is necessary that one part is true and the other false — i.e., although the disjunctive is true — nevertheless neither part is determinately true or determinately false. The Philosopher's whole meaning, therefore, is that as regards future contingents neither part is determinately* true or false, as the thing itself is determined neither to be going to be nor to be going not to be.

It is evident, therefore, that it is not necessary that one of the opposites belonging to
every affirmation or negation is true but the other false. For it is not the same with
things that are as with those that are not but possibly are or are not; how it is with
them has already been said. (19a39–19b4)

[In part 9.222] he infers two corollaries. The first is that it is not always necessary that one part of a contradiction is true and the other false. The second corollary is that the parts of a contradiction involving propositions about the future are not related to truth and falsity in the same way as are the parts of a contradiction involving propositions about the present or about the past.

For a clear understanding of this entire chapter it must be known, first, that it is the Philosopher's view that neither part of a contradiction involving such future contingents is determinately* true or false, as the [corresponding] thing is determined no more to be going to be than to be going not to be. Thus he would say that God does not know one part of such* a contradiction more than the other; indeed, neither is known by God. For from the fact that neither part is true (as he shows here) and that nothing is known except what is true (according to him in Book One of the *Posterior*

Analytics [Ch. 2, 71b26]), it follows that neither part is known. Yet it must be said otherwise in accordance with truth and the theologians, for it must be said that God determinately knows one or the other part. But how He does so must be explained in theology.

In the second place it must be known that from the Philosopher's point of view it is not only sometimes as regards propositions verbally about the future that neither part [of a contradiction] is determinately true, but also sometimes as regards those [verbally] about the present and about the past. And this is the case when one about the past or about the present is equivalent to one about the future. For example, the two propositions '*A* will be' and '*A* is something future' seem equivalent (and the same is true as regards many others); therefore one of them is no more true than the other. (I am not now concerned, however, with the question of whether or not such propositions are equivalent taken literally.)

In the third place it must be known that nothing of which the Philosopher speaks here is fortuitously contingent except what is in the power of someone acting freely or what depends on such an agent. Therefore in pure natural things—i.e., in animate things only the sensitive soul, and in [all] inanimate things—there is no contingency, nor any chance or fortune, unless they depend in some way on a free agent. In all the other things of which the Philosopher speaks here, however, there is inevitability and necessity.

Nor does what is said in Book Two of the *Physics* [Ch. 6, 197b1-197b22] conflict [with this]—viz., that there is chance in inanimate things and fortune in animate things—for although chance may be found in inanimate things, it nevertheless comes from a source that depends on some free agent. Therefore if the action of an agent was free neither in itself nor in respect of some source [outside itself] there will be no chance, but it will come about of necessity (which is how Book Two of the *Physics* is to be explained).[26]

Because of what has been said so far it is clear that the Philosopher would concede this consequence: 'God knows that *A* will be; therefore *A* will be.' But he would say that the antecedent is simply false and the consequent is neither true nor false. Nor is it an ab-

[26]Cf. Appendix I, p. 89.

surdity that what is neither true nor false should follow from what
is false, just as what is true follows from what is false.

But is this consequence acceptable: '*A* will be; therefore God
knows that *A* will be'? Perhaps the Philosopher would say that the
consequence does not hold since the proposition '*A* will be'—i.e.,
the antecedent*—is neither true nor false and the consequent is
simply false and therefore the consequence does not hold.

And suppose one says that since the consequence does not
hold the opposite of the consequent is consistent with the antecedent, and consequently '*A* will be' and 'God does not know that *A*
will be' are consistent. But this is impossible, since it is impossible
that these are true together. For if '*A* will be' and 'God does not
know that *A* will be' are true together, then 'something true is not
known by God' is possible, which seems impossible.

In response to all this perhaps the Philosopher would say that
[the claim that] two* propositions are consistent can be taken in two
ways. In one way [it means] that they can be true together, and '*A*
will be' and 'God does not know that *A* will be' are not consistent in
that sense. In the other way [it means] that neither implies the
opposite of the other, and in that sense they are consistent.

From this it is clear that from the Philosopher's point of view
this consequence does not hold good: 'it is impossible that the antecedent is true without the consequent; therefore the consequence
is acceptable.' For example, in the case before us it is impossible
that the proposition '*A* will be' is true without the proposition 'God
knows that *A* will be,' and yet the consequence '*A* will be; therefore
God knows that *A* will be' does not hold. Nevertheless when the
antecedent and the consequent are determinately true or determinately false, or if one is determinately true and the other determinately false, the consequence holds good.

It must also be noted, in the fourth place,* that from the Philosopher's point of view a universal affirmative [proposition] is true
although no singular [proposition belonging to it] is true. For example, according to him 'every future contingent will be' is determinately true,[27] and yet no singular [belonging to it] is true, since
for whatever singular is picked out 'this future contingent will be' is

[27]Cf. Appendix III, pp. 111–113. Both this passage and the related longer passage in Appendix III are obscure. Two different points [(1) and (2)] might have

not true, for that implies 'this will be,' which, according to the Philosopher, is neither true nor false.

Then what is required for the truth of such a universal? It must be said that according to the Philosopher what is required is the truth of the various* disjunctive propositions composed of the parts of the contradiction. Thus if 'every future contingent will be' is true it requires that 'this future contingent either will be or will not be' is true, and so on with regard to the singulars. Nor is it more absurd that such a universal should be true while no singular belonging to it is true than that a disjunctive should be true although neither part is true. This is the special case of propositions that do not have determinate truth or falsity.

Therefore many general rules must be denied in this subject matter, since according to the Philosopher they have a counterinstance here. For example, the rule 'the consequence from a universal proposition to a singular [belonging to it] is acceptable,' [or] 'a universal [proposition] is sufficiently inferred by induction on the basis of [all] the singulars belonging to it' takes a counterinstance.[28]

---

been raised here by Ockham against Aristotle, each of which bears some resemblance to what is actually said in these passages. (1) Aristotle wants to allow for the truth of such universal disjunctive propositions as 'for every future contingent, either it will be or it will not be.' Suppose that A is a future contingent. Then the disjunctive 'either A will be or A will not be' is true. But a disjunctive is true if and only if one of its disjuncts is true, and, according to Aristotle, neither of these disjuncts is true (since neither is true or false). (2) Aristotle wants to allow for the determinate truth or falsity of universal propositions about the future while denying determinate truth or falsity of singular propositions about the future. The universal proposition 'every future contingent will be' is, according to Aristotle, either true or false (in fact false). But a universal proposition is true if and only if each singular proposition belonging to it is true, and a universal proposition is false if and only if at least one singular proposition belonging to it is false. Therefore, since 'every future contingent will be' is either true or false, either each singular proposition belonging to it is true or at least one singular proposition belonging to it is false. But, according to Aristotle, *none* of the singular propositions belonging to it is *either* true or false.

[28]The first of these two rules is evidently violated in the consequence 'every future contingent will be; therefore this future contingent will be,' for the antecedent can be true and, whether or not it is true, the consequent is not true (since it is neither true nor false). The second rule may be taken to have been violated if it is read as a claim that the truth-value of a universal proposition is determinable on the basis of an exhaustive investigation of the truth-values of all the singular propositions belonging to it. But the discovery that 'this future contingent will be' (and each such singular proposition) is not true (since it is neither true nor false) does not warrant the conclusion that 'no future contingent will be' is true.

For the consequence 'this future contingent will not be, that future contingent will not be (and so on with regard to the singulars); therefore no future contingent will be' does not hold, for the consequent is determinately false and the antecedent is not determinately false; therefore the consequence does not hold. And as it is with these, so it is with many others, for an exactly similar reason.

APPENDIX III

Summa logicae, Part III–3, Chapter 32 (in part)

But as regards the induction of a universal proposition about the future, the first thing to know is that the induction of a necessary or an impossible proposition about the future is to be described in the same way as the induction of such propositions about the present or about the past. The induction of a universal proposition about the future in contingent matter,[29] however, is to be described in one way in accordance with truth and the Faith* and in another way in accordance with Aristotle's point of view. This difference arises from the fact that one must be of one opinion about the truth of a contingent proposition about the future in accordance with truth and the Faith and of another opinion in accordance with Aristotle's point of view.

For Aristotle maintains that no such contingent proposition about the future is either true or false; thus in accordance with Aristotle's point of view one part of a contradiction involving such propositions is no more true than the other. Therefore, according to him, one part of [such] a contradiction is no more known by any intellect whatever than is the other, for what is no more true [than another] is no more knowable [than another]. For this reason Aristotle would not have maintained that a future contingent is known by God, since in his view no future contingent is true, and nothing is known except what is true.

The truth of the Faith maintains, however, that future contingents are known by God, so that one part of a contradiction [involving them] is known by God and the other is not known by

---

[29]The distinction of propositions on the basis of their "matter" is parallel to but not identical with the distinction of them on the basis of modalities. Cf. William of Sherwood: "It should also be noted that the matter of statements is of three kinds, viz., natural, contingent, and separate . . . [as in] 'a man is an animal' . . . 'a man is running'. . . . 'a man is an ass' " (Kretzmann, *William of Sherwood's Introduction to Logic,* p. 33).

110

God. For example, from eternity God knew this: the Blessed Virgin is to be saved, and never knew this: the Blessed Virgin is not to be saved, just as He did not ever know this: the Blessed Virgin is to be damned. Therefore one part of the contradiction is known and not the other; and so one part is true — viz., the one that is known — and the other is not true, since it is not known by God.

Thus from Aristotle's point of view a universal affirmative about the future could be true even though no singular [proposition belonging to it] is true. For example, according to him the universal proposition 'every future contingent will be' is true (indeed, according to him it is necessary), and yet in his view no singular proposition belonging to it is true. For, according to him, whichever one is picked out, 'this future contingent will be' is not true, for it implies 'this is something future [and] contingent,' which according to him is neither true nor false any more than is 'this is something future,' which it implies.

Similarly, in his view a universal proposition about the future could be false even though it does not have any false singular proposition [belonging to it]. For example, the universal proposition 'no future contingent will be' is false, and yet it does not have any false singular proposition [belonging to it]. For, according to him, whichever one is picked out, 'this future contingent will not be' is not a [false] singular proposition belonging to it,[30] for the reason given above.

And just as sometimes such a universal* affirmative is true although no singular [belonging to it is true], so, according to him, sometimes a particular affirmative is true although no singular [belonging to it] is true. On this basis he would solve such arguments as these. That 'Socrates will be tomorrow' is true is proved in the following way. 'At some instant Socrates will be' is true. And, according to him, this proposition must be granted if Socrates is; for he supposes that there is no last instant (*ultimum*) of a real thing's enduring in being.[31] Therefore if 'at some instant Socrates will be' is true (let that instant be t_1), then 'Socrates will be at t_1' is

[30]In virtue of its form alone it is a singular proposition belonging to 'no future contingent will be,' but (since it is neither true nor false) it is not true.

[31]On the medieval treatment of beginning and ceasing, particularly in connection with the verbs '*incipit*' (begins) and '*desinit*', see Norman Kretzmann, "Incipit/Desinit" in P. K. Machamer and R. G. Turnbull, eds., *Motion and Time, Space and Matter* (Columbus, Ohio: Ohio State University Press, 1976), pp. 101–136. For Ockham's discussions of '*incipit*' and '*desinit*' see *Summa logicae* I 75 and II 19.

true. Moreover, therefore he will be at some instant after t_1 (let this be granted and let that instant be t_2). And the argument proceeds as before—therefore he will be at some instant after t_2, since otherwise t_2 would be his last instant, which is not possible. In the same way this follows: 'Socrates will be at t_2; therefore he will be at some instant after t_2' (let this be granted and let that instant be t_3). And in this way finally the next day will be arrived at.

In response to this the Philosopher would say that 'at some instant Socrates will be' is true but no singular belonging to it is true, and so the instant at which Socrates will be must not be given. Thus according to him 'at some instant Socrates will be' is true and yet none of these is true: 'at t_1 Socrates will be,' 'at t_2 Socrates will be,' and so on with regard to the singular [propositions belonging to that particular proposition]. And so none of these is to be given. Moreover, from his point of view similar arguments must be responded to in the same way.[32]

But in accordance with the truth of the Faith, if such a universal affirmative is true and known by God it does have a true singular [proposition belonging to it], and this is because it is always the case that one or the other part of a contradiction is true and known by God.

It should be noted, however, that sometimes a universal or a particular [proposition] is true in one way and a singular [proposition belonging to one of them is true] in another way. For on one view a universal is necessary although no singular [belonging to it] is necessary; indeed, any and every [such] singular is true in such a way that it can be false and can never have been true. For 'any and every true future contingent is true' is necessary although no singular [belonging to it] is true except in such a way that it could never have been true.[33] Similarly, it can (*poterit*) be that a particular proposition is inevitably true although any and every singular [belonging to it] is avoidably true. (And in this re-

---

[32]Ockham's example seems unnecessarily complicated. 'Some future contingent will be' would apparently have served his principal purposes better than 'at some instant Socrates will be.'

[33]This example, too, is confusing, perhaps in part because of unnecessary complication. By a singular belonging to the universal 'any and every true future contingent is true' he should mean 'this true future contingent is true.' The point seems to be that, despite its look of analyticity, the singular is not true because there is no instance satisfying the description in the subject term. The singular proposition may

spect there is a certain resemblance between Aristotle's view and the truth of the Faith.)

What has been said regarding propositions about the future must also be said regarding propositions about the past and about the present that are equivalent to propositions about the future. Thus 'he will be saved' is true although it is possible that it will never have been true. For this follows: 'he will commit the sin of final impenitence; therefore he will be damned,' and further 'therefore he will not be saved,' and further "therefore 'he will be saved' never was true." The antecedent is possible (as is evident), and so the consequent is possible. In the same way 'he was predestinate from eternity' is now true although it is possible that he will never have been predestinate. This is because 'he was predestinate from eternity' is equivalent to the proposition 'he will be saved,' which is about the future. And so just as the one can never have been true, so it is possible that the other will never have been true.

And this is the difference between the truth of propositions about the future and of those equivalent to them and the truth of propositions about the past and about the present that are not equivalent to those about the future; for if a proposition is true about the present, then necessarily it will always be true afterwards to say that that proposition was true. For example, if 'Socrates is seated' is true now, then "'Socrates is seated' was true" will always be necessary afterwards, so that it is impossible that the entire proposition "'Socrates is seated' was true" should ever be false afterwards. Similarly as regards a proposition about the past. For if 'Socrates was white' is true now, then "'Socrates was white' was true" will always be necessary afterwards. But it is otherwise as regards a proposition about the future. For however true 'John will be saved' is now, nevertheless "'John will be saved' was true" will be contingent afterwards.

On this basis one can show that predestination or reprobation or anything of that sort cannot be a real relation inhering in the predestinate or reprobate creature, as some maintain. For if it were

---

be analyzed as a conjunction: 'this is a true future contingent and this is true.' On the view under discussion the first conjunct is invariably false, and hence the conjunction is invariably false. (The analyticity of the original singular proposition shows up in the fact that if the first conjunct were true the second conjunct would be true.)

such a thing it would follow that he who is predestinate could not be damned. For if predestination is such a thing, then 'he is predestinate because of such a thing inhering in himself' will be true, just as 'Socrates is white because of whiteness inhering in him' is true. Consequently "'he is predestinate' was true" will afterwards be necessary, and if that is the case it follows that 'he will be saved' is now necessary. For this follows: "it is necessary that 'he is predestinate' was true; therefore he will be saved." And the antecedent is necessary, and so the consequent is necessary. From this it follows that 'he will be saved' is now necessary.

On this basis one can also show that if some contingent is true at some instant it can in no way be false at that same instant. For example, if 'he performs a good act' is true now, then it is impossible that 'he performs a good act' is false at this instant. The reason for this is that what is necessary must never be denied as the result of the positing in reality of what is possible. But if it is posited in reality that he sins, then " 'he performs a good act at t_1' was true," which is necessary after this instant, must be denied. Consequently, if t_1 is occurring and he is performing a good act at t_1, then 'he does not perform a good act at t_1' is impossible. Nevertheless before [t_1] it was possible. But as a result of the fact that it is posited in actuality, that is no longer possible.

> N.B. The critical edition of Ockham's philosophical and theological works published by The Franciscan Institute of St. Bonaventure University in a series of volumes beginning in 1967 supplants every edition cited in this book.

BIBLIOGRAPHIES

The following five lists are intended primarily as aids to further study and are not complete bibliographies. (More extensive lists can be found in Heynck, Valens. "Ockham-Literatur 1919-1949," *Franziskanische Studien*, XXXII (1950), pp. 164-183; Vasoli, Cesare. "Bibliografia," pp. 301-332 in his book designated 2.23 below; and in several other general works in List 2.) In order to enhance the usefulness of these lists we cite English translations and works in English wherever possible. An asterisk before the numerical designation indicates that the work is referred to in our notes.

1. OCKHAM'S NONPOLITICAL WORKS IN PROBABLE CHRONOLOGICAL ORDER

[Detailed information regarding manuscripts, editions, and evidence of chronological order can be found in several bibliographies. For example, Boehner, Philotheus. "A Bibliography on Ockham," pp. 16-23 in edition cited in 2.5 below; Brampton, C. K. "The Probable Order of Ockham's Non-Polemical Works," *Traditio*, XIX (1963), pp. 469-483. We indicate available English translations in this list, using these abbreviations: (B) Boehner, Philotheus (ed. and tr.). *Ockham: Philosophical Writ-*

ings. [Latin and English.] Edinburgh: Thomas Nelson and Sons, 1957; (S) Shapiro, Herman. *Medieval Philosophy. Selected Readings from Augustine to Buridan.* New York: Modern Library, 1964. [Translations taken from B.]; (M) McKeon, Richard. *Selections from Medieval Philosophers. II. Roger Bacon to William Ockham.* New York: Scribners, 1930; (T) Tornay, Stephen Chak. *Ockham, Studies and Selections.* La Salle, Ill.: Open Court, 1938; (HW) Hyman, Arthur, and Walsh, James J. *Philosophy in the Middle Ages.* New York: Harper & Row, 1967 [some translations taken from B]; (AK) the present volume.]

1.1 *Prima redactio* [First version of Book One of his *Commentary on the Sentences* of Peter Lombard.]

1.2 *Reportatio* [Books II–IV of his *Commentary on the Sentences.*]

       Book II, Q. xv (HW, pp. 626–635)

       Book II, Q. xxvi, **N** ff. (B, pp. 139–141)

       Book III, Q. viii. (B, pp. 106–113)

       Book III, Q. xii (HW, pp. 645–652)

*1.3 *Ordinatio* [Second version of Book One of his *Commentary on the Sentences.*]

       Prologus, Q. i, **N** ff. (B, pp. 18–25; S)

       D. II, Q. iv (HW, pp. 618–624)

       D. II, Q. vi (HW, pp. 624–626)

       D. II, Q. viii, **E–F** (B, pp. 41–43; S)

       D. II, Q. ix, **P** ff. (B, pp. 102–106)

       D. III, Q. ii, **E–M.** (T, pp. 182–187)

       D. XXX, Q. i (HW, pp. 635–642)

       D. XXXV, Q. v. (T, pp. 137–164)

       D. XXXVIII, Q. unica. (AK); **L–N.** (B, pp. 133–135)

       D. XXXIX, Q. unica. (AK)

1.4 *Expositio in librum Porphyrii*

1.5 *Expositio in librum Praedicamentorum*

*1.6 *Expositio in duos libros Perihermenias*

       Prooemium [in part]. (B, pp. 43–45)

       Chapter 9. (AK)

1.7 *Expositio in duos libros Elenchorum*

1.8 *Tractatus de sacramento altaris*

*1.9 *Tractatus de praedestinatione et de praescientia Dei et de futuris contingentibus*

       [Complete]. (AK)

1.10 *Expositio super octo libros Physicorum*
      Prologus. (B, pp. 2-16)
*1.11 *Summa totius logicae*
        I, c. i. (B, pp. 47-49; HW; T, 91-94)
          c. ii. (B, pp. 49-51; T, 94-96)
          c. iv. (B, pp. 51-52; HW)
          c. x. (B, pp. 52-56; HW)
          c. xi. (B, pp. 56-58; HW; T, 96-99)
          c. xii. (T, pp. 99-102)
          c. xiii. (B, pp. 59-62)
          c. xiv. (B, pp. 32-34; S)
          c. xv. (B, pp. 35-37; S)
          c. xvi. (B, pp. 37-40; S)
          c. xxxviii. (B, pp. 90-92)
          c. xli. (T, pp. 102-106)
          c. xliii. (T, pp. 106-112)
          c. xliv. (B, pp. 137-139)
          c. lxii. (B, pp. 64-65; HW)
          c. lxiii. (B, pp. 65-68; HW; T, 113-115)
          c. lxiv. (B, pp. 68-70; T, 115-118)
          c. lxvii. (B, pp. 70-74)
      II, c. ii. (B, pp. 76-78; HW)
          c. xxxi. (B, pp. 80-81)
          c. xxxii. (B, pp. 81-82)
    III, I, c. i. (B, pp. 83-84)
       II, c. xxvii. (B, pp. 92-95)
       III, c. xxxii. (AK)
          c. xxxvi. (B, pp. 84-88)
*1.12 *Summulae in libros Physicorum* [or *Philosophia naturalis*]
*1.13 *Quodlibeta VII*
        I, Q. i. (B, pp. 125-126)
          Q. x. (B, pp. 141-144)
          Q. xiii. (B, pp. 27-32; S; M, 360-366)
          Q. xiv. (M, pp. 395-398)
          Q. xv. (M, pp. 366-368)
      II, Q. x. (M, pp. 398-403)
          Q. xii. (M, pp. 393-395)
          Q. xiii. (M, pp. 403-411)
    III, Q. iii. (B, pp. 128-132)

2. RECENT DISCUSSIONS OF RELEVANT ASPECTS OF OCKHAM'S PHILOSOPHY

*2.1 Adams, Marilyn McCord. "The Problem of God's Foreknowledge and Free Will in Boethius and William Ockham." Unpublished Ph.D. dissertation, Cornell University, 1967.

 2.2 Baudry, Leon. *Guillaume d'Occam. Sa vie, ses oeuvres, ses idees sociales et politiques. Tome I: L'homme et les oeuvres.* ("Etudes de Philosophie Médiévale," *XXXIX*). Paris: J. Vrin, 1949.

*2.3   — — —. *Lexique philosophique de Guillaume d'Ockham. Étude des notions fondamentales.* Paris: P. Lethielleux, 1958.

*2.4 Boehner, Philotheus. "Introduction," pp. ix-xi in his edition *The Tractatus de Praedestinatione et de Praescientia Dei et de Futuris Contingentibus of William Ockham. Edited with a Study on the Mediaeval Problem of a Three-Valued Logic.* ("Franciscan Institute Publications" No. 2). St. Bonaventure, N.Y.: The Franciscan Institute, 1945.

*2.5   — — —. "Introductory," pp. 1-23 in his edition *The Tractatus de Successivis Attributed to William Ockham. Edited with a Study on the Life and Works of Ockham.* ("Franciscan Institute Publications" No. 1). St. Bonaventure, N.Y.: The Franciscan Institute, 1944.

*2.6 — — —. "Ockham's *Tractatus de Praedestinatione et de Praescientia Dei et de Futuris Contingentibus* and its Main Problems," *Proceedings of the American Catholic Philosophical Association,* XVI (1941), pp. 177–192. Reprinted in Boehner, Philotheus. *Collected Articles on Ockham,* Edited by Eligius M. Buytaert. ("Franciscan Institute Publications, Philosophy Series" No. 12). St. Bonaventure, N.Y.: The Franciscan Institute, 1958.

2.7 — — —. "Problems Connected with the *Tractatus*," pp. 43–88 in edition cited in 2.4.

*2.8 — — —. "Der Stand der Ockham-Forschung," *Franziskanische Studien,* XXXIV (1952), pp. 12–31. Reprinted in collection cited in 2.6.

*2.9 — — —. "The Text Tradition of Ockham's *Ordinatio*," *The New Scholasticism,* XVI (1942), pp. 203–221. Reprinted in collection cited in 2.6.

2.10 — — —. "On a Recent Study of Ockham," *Franciscan Studies,* X (1950), pp. 191–196. Reprinted in collection cited in 2.6. [Discussion of 2.16]

2.11 Boh, Ivan. "An Examination of Ockham's Aretetic Logic," *Archiv für die Geschichte der Philosophie,* XLV (1963), pp. 259–268.

2.12 Copleston, Frederick. *A History of Philosophy.* Vol. III, "Late Medieval and Renaissance Philosophy," Part I, "Ockham to the Speculative Mystics," Chapter 6, Sections 5–7, pp. 100–107. Garden City, N.Y.: Doubleday Image Books, 1963.

2.13 González, Anselmo. "Guillermo de Ockham, *De praedestinatione*: Introduccion de Anselmo González," *Ideas y Valores,* VI (1963–64), pp. 303–360.

2.14 Iserloh, Erwin. *Gnade und Eucharistie in der philosophischen Theologie des Wilhelm von Ockham.* (Especially pp. 44–133.) Wiesbaden: Franz Steiner, 1956.

2.15 — — —. "Um die Echtheit des 'Centiloquium': Ein Beitrag zur Wertung Ockhams und zur Chronologie seiner Werke (II)," *Gregorianum,* XXX (1949), pp. 309–346.

2.16 Maier, Anneliese. "Die Subjektivierung der Zeit in der scholastischen Philosophie," *Philosophia Naturalis,* I (1951), pp. 361–398.

*2.17 Menges, Matthew C. *The Concept of Univocity Regarding the Predication of God and Creature According to William Ockham.* ("Franciscan Institute Publications, Philosophy Series" No. 9). St. Bonaventure, N.Y.: The Franciscan Institute, 1952.

2.18 Moody, Ernest A. "William of Ockham," *The Encyclopedia of Philosophy,* ed. Edwards, P., Vol. VIII, pp. 306–317. New York: The Macmillan Co. and The Free Press, 1967.

2.19 Moser, Simon. *Grundbegriffe der Naturphilosophie bei Wilhelm von Ockham.* (Especially Part IV, "Die Zeit"). Innsbruck: Felizian Rauch, 1932.

2.20 Pelster, Franz. "Die Lehre Ockhams vom Grund der Möglichkeit bei Possibilien," *Scholastik,* XXVIII (1953), pp. 405–407. [Discussion of 2.27]

2.21 Prior, Arthur N. [Same as 5.27 below].

2.22 Shapiro, Herman. *Motion, Time and Place According to William Ockham.* ("Franciscan Institute Publications, Philosophy Series" No. 13). St. Bonaventure, N.Y.: The Franciscan Institute, 1957.

2.23 Tweedale, Martin. "Scotus and Ockham on the Infinity of the Most Eminent Being," *Franciscan Studies,* XXIII (1963), pp. 257–267.

2.24 Vasoli, Cesare. *Guglielmo d'Occam.* (Especially Chapter VI, Parts 2 and 3.) Firenze: La Nuova Italia, 1953.

2.25 Vignaux, Paul. *Justification et prédestination au XIVe siècle. Duns Scot, Pierre d'Auriole, Guillaume d'Ockham, Gregoire de Rimini.* ("Bibliotheque de l'ecole des Hautes Études, Sciences religieuses" tome 48). Paris: Ernest Leroux, 1934.

2.26 – – –. "Sur Luther et Ockham," *Franziskanische Studien,* XXXII (1950), pp. 21–30.

2.27 Wolter, Allan B. "Ockham and the Textbooks: On the Origin of Possibility," *Franziskanishe Studien,* XXXII (1950), pp. 70–96.

3. OTHER MEDIEVAL PHILOSOPHERS ON TOPICS CLOSELY RELATED TO THOSE DISCUSSED IN OCKHAM'S *TREATISE*

[List 3 contains works on or by some philosophers whose treatment of these topics is important historically or influential on

Ockham. Besides other treatises devoted specifically to these topics there are countless medieval commentaries on Aristotle's *De interpretatione* and on Peter Lombard's *Sentences*, any one of which is likely to contain relevant discussions.]

*3.1 Alexander of Hales. *Summa theologica.* Quaracchi: Typographia Collegii S. Bonaventurae, 1924. Pars I, Inq. I, Tract. V, Sect. II, Q. I (pp. 266–275); Q. III, Tit. I (pp. 281–304); Q. IV, Tit. I–IV (pp. 315–345).

*3.2 Anselm of Canterbury. *On the Harmony of the Foreknowledge, the Predestination, and the Grace of God with Free Choice* in *Anselm of Canterbury: Theological Treatises*, ed. Hopkins, Jasper and Richardson, Herbert (tr. Johnson, Kane, Phyles, and Waldrop). Vol. III, pp. 47–100. Cambridge: Harvard Divinity School Library, 1967.

3.3 – – –. *On Freedom of Choice* in *Anselm of Canterbury: Truth, Freedom, and Evil*, ed. and tr. Hopkins, Jasper and Richardson, Herbert. Pp. 121–144. New York: Harper & Row, 1967.

3.4 – – –. *Monologion*, Chapters 21–22; pp. 73–81 in *St. Anselm: Basic Writings*, tr. Deane, S. N. La Salle, Ill.: Open Court, 1903.

3.5 – – –. *Proslogion*, Chapter 19; pp. 141–143 in *St. Anselm's Proslogion*, tr. Charlesworth, M. J. [Latin and English.] Oxford: Clarendon Press, 1965.

3.6 Augustine of Hippo. *Contra epistolam Manichaei quam vocant Fundamenti* in *A Select Library of the Nicene and Post-Nicene Fathers of the Christian Church*, ed. Schaff, P. Vol. IV, pp. 129–130. Grand Rapids, Mich.: W. B. Eerdmans, 1956.

3.7 – – –. *Contra Faustum Manichaeum* in series cited in 3.6; Vol. IV, pp. 155–345.

3.8 – – –. *De civitate Dei* [*The City of God*], Book V, Chapters 9–11; pp. 64–70 in *Basic Writings of Saint Augustine*, ed. Oates, W. J., Vol. II. New York: Random House, 1948.

3.9 – – –. *De dono perseverantiae* [*On the Gift of Perseverance*] in series cited in 3.6; Vol. V, pp. 521–552.

3.10 – – –. *De gratia et libero arbitrio* [*On Grace and Free Will*] in collection cited in 3.8; Vol. I, pp. 733–774.

3.11 – – –. *De libero arbitrio* [*On Free Choice of the Will*], tr. Benjamin, A. S. and Hackstaff, L. H. New York: Library of Liberal Arts, 1964.

3.12 ‒ ‒ ‒. *Of the Morals of the Catholic Church*, Chapters 3, 4, 5, 11, 12, 14; pp. 163‒168 in *Selected Writings of St. Augustine*, ed. Hazelton, Roger. New York: World Publishing Co., 1962.

3.13 ‒ ‒ ‒. *De natura et gratia* [*On Nature and Grace*], Chapters 3‒5, 49‒59; in collection cited in 3.8; Vol. I, pp. 523‒524; 553‒559.

3.14 ‒ ‒ ‒. *De praedestinatione Dei* in Migne, J. P. *Patrologia latina*, Vol. XLV, cols. 1677‒1678.

3.15 ‒ ‒ ‒. *De praedestinatione et gratia* in Migne, J. P. *Patrologia latina*, Vol. XLV, cols. 1665‒1676.

3.16 ‒ ‒ ‒. *De praedestinatione sanctorum* [*On the Predestination of the Saints*] in collection cited in 3.8; Vol. I, pp. 777‒817.

3.17 ‒ ‒ ‒. *On Rebuke and Grace*, Chapters 31‒34; in collection cited in 3.12, pp. 212‒215.

3.18 ‒ ‒ ‒. *De trinitate* [*On the Trinity*], Book XV; in collection cited in 3.8; Vol. II, pp. 830‒878.

3.19 ‒ ‒ ‒. *De utilitate credendi* [*On the Profit of Believing*] in collection cited in 3.8; Vol. I, pp. 399‒427.

3.20 ‒ ‒ ‒. *Enarratio in psalmum XLIX* in collection cited in 3.6; Vol. VIII, pp. 169‒177.

3.21 ‒ ‒ ‒. *Enchiridion*, Chapters XCVII‒CVII; in collection cited in 3.8; Vol. I, pp. 714‒722.

3.22 ‒ ‒ ‒. *Letter 217* in collection cited in 3.12; pp. 216‒221.

3.23 ‒ ‒ ‒. *Sermo XXVI* in collection cited in 3.6; Vol. VI, pp. 340‒342.

3.24 Baudry, Léon. "La préscience divine chez S. Anselme," *Archives d'Histoire Doctrinale et Littéraire du Moyen Age*, XVII (1942), pp. 223‒237.

3.25 ‒ ‒ ‒. *La querelle des futurs contingents (Louvain 1465‒1475). Textes inédits.* ("Études de Philosophie Médiévale" XXXVIII). Paris: J. Vrin, 1950.

*3.26 ‒ ‒ ‒. *Le Tractatus de principiis theologiae attribué à G. d'Occam.* ("Études de Philosophie Médiévale," XXIII). Paris: J. Vrin, 1936.

*3.27 Boethius. *De consolatione philosophiae* [*The Consolation of Philosophy*], pp. 128‒411 in *Boethius. The Theological Tractates and The Consolation of Philosophy.* ("The Loeb Classical Library"). Cambridge, Mass.: Harvard University Press, 1953.

3.28 — — —. *In librum Aristotelis De interpretatione* (2 vols.), ed.
      Meiser, C. ("Bibliotheca scriptorum graecorum et romano-
      rum Teubneriana"). Leipzig: Teubner, 1877–1880.

*3.29 Bonansea, Bernardine M. "Duns Scotus' Voluntarism," pp.
      83–121 in *John Duns Scotus, 1265–1965*, ed. Ryan, J. K. and
      Bonansea, B. M. ("Studies in Philosophy and the History of
      Philosophy" Vol. 3). Washington, D.C.: Catholic University
      of America Press, 1965.

*3.30 Duns Scotus. *Opus Oxoniense (Ordinatio)* I, d. XXXVIII–XLI
      in *Opera omnia*, Vol. VI, pp. 303–339. Civitas Vaticana:
      Typis Polyglottia Vaticanis, 1963.

*3.31 — — —. *Opus Parisiense (Reportatio; Reportata Parisiensia)* I, d.
      XXXVIII–XLI.

3.32 Gregory of Rimini. *Lectura in primum Sententiarum*, d. 38, q.
      1. Appendix V, pp. 125–138 in Boehner edition cited in 2.4
      above.

*3.33 Groblicki, J. *De scientia Dei futurorum contingentium secundum
      S. Thomam ejusque primos sequaces.* ("Editiones Facultatis
      Theologiae Universitatis Cracoviensis," Series I, No. 30).
      Cracow: University Press, 1938.

*3.34 Isaac, J. *Le Peri Hermeneias en occident de Boèce à Saint Thomas.*
      ("Bibliotheque Thomiste," XXIX). Paris: J. Vrin, 1953.

3.35 John of Ripa. *Conclusiones circa primum librum Sententiarum*,
      d. XXXVIII, Q. II, 1–4 (pp. 229–231); d. XXXIX, Q. I, 1–4
      (pp. 232–237); d. XL, Q. I–II (pp. 238–243); d. XLI (pp.
      244–246). *Conclusiones circa secundum librum Sententiarum*, Q.
      1, 1–4 (pp. 267–272). ("Etudes de Philosophie Medievale,"
      XLIV). Paris: J. Vrin, 1957.

3.36 Oesterle, Jean T. *Aristotle: On Interpretation. Commentary by St.
      Thomas and Cajetan.* ("Medieval Philosophical Texts in
      Translation," No. 11). Milwaukee, Wisc.: Marquette Univer-
      sity Press, 1962.

3.37 Pannenberg, Wolfhart. *Die Prädestinationslehre des Duns Sko-
      tus im Zusammenhang der scholastichen Lehrentwicklung*, Göttin-
      gen: Vandenhoeck und Ruprecht, 1954. [Includes bibliog-
      raphy].

3.38 Peter Abelard. *Dialectica*, Tractatus secundus, II, 8–11; pp.
      210–222; ed. De Rijk, L. M. Assen: Van Gorcum, 1956.

3.39 Peter Auriol. *In primum Sententiarum*, d. 38, art. 3. Appendix
      IV, pp. 118-124, in Boehner edition cited in 2.4 above.
3.40 Peter Lombard. *Sententiarum libri quatuor*, Lib. I, d.
      XXXVIII-XL. in Migne, J. P. *Patrologia latina*, Vol. CXCII,
      cols. 626-633.
3.41 Proclus. "On Providence and Faith," pp. 483-485 in *The Six
      Books of Proclus*, tr. Taylor, T. London: Longman and Co.,
      1816.
3.42 Rowe, William L. "St. Augustine on Foreknowledge and
      Free Will," *The Review of Metaphysics*, XVII (1963-64), pp.
      356-363.
3.43 Schmaus, Michael. "Des Petrus de Trabibus Lehre über das
      göttliche Vorauswissen und die Prädestination," *Antonia-
      num*, X (1935), pp. 121-148.
3.44 – – –. "Guilelmi de Alnwick OFM doctrina de medio quo
      Deus cognoscit futura contingentia," *Bogoslovni Vestnik*, XII
      (1932), pp. 201-255.
3.45 – – –. "Uno sconosciuto discepolo di Scoto. Intorno alla
      prescienza di Dio," *Rivista di filiosofia neo-scolastica*, XXIV
      (1932), pp. 327-355.
3.46 Schwamm, Hermann. *Magistri Ioannis de Ripa OFM doctrina
      de praescientia divina*. ("Analecta Gregorianna" Fasciculus I).
      Romae: In Pontificia Universitate Gregoriana, 1930.
3.47 – – –. *Robert Cowton OFM über das gottliche Vorherwissen*.
      ("Philosophie und Grenzwissenschaften" Band III, Heft 5).
      Innsbruck: Felizian Rauch, 1930.
3.48 Thomas Aquinas. *Quaestiones disputatae de veritate [Disputed
      Questions on Truth]*, Q. V-VI, in *Thomas Aquinas: Providence
      and Predestination*, tr. Mulligan, R. W. Chicago: Henry W.
      Regnery Co., 1961.
3.49 – – –. *Summa contra gentiles [On the Truth of the Catholic
      Faith]*, Book One, Chapter 67 (Vol. I, pp. 221-225); Book
      Three (complete); tr. Pegis, A. C. and Bourke, V. J. Garden
      City, N.Y.: Doubleday Image Books, 1955.
3.50 – – –. *Summa theologica*, Part I, Q. 14, art. 13 (Vol. I, pp.
      154-157); Q. 22 (pp. 229-237); Q. 23 (pp. 238-251); Q.
      82-83 (pp. 777-792); Part I-II, Q. 6-21 (Vol. II, pp.
      225-364); Q. 109-114 (pp. 919-1050) in *Basic Writings of
      Saint Thomas Aquinas*, ed. Pegis, A. C. New York: Random
      House, 1945.

4. RECENT DISCUSSIONS OF TOPICS CLOSELY RELATED TO THOSE DISCUSSED IN OCKHAM'S *TREATISE*

4.1 Adams, Marilyn McCord. "Is the Existence of God a 'Hard' Fact?" *Philosophical Review*, LXXVI (1967), pp. 492–503. [Discussion of 4.7, 4.14, 4.8].

4.2 Castañeda, Hector-Neri. "Omniscience and Indexical Reference," *The Journal of Philosophy*, LXIV (1967), pp. 203–209. [Discussion of 4.5].

*4.3 Flew, Antony. "Precognition," *The Encyclopedia of Philosophy*, ed. Edwards, P., Vol. VI, pp. 436–441. New York: The Macmillan Co. and The Free Press, 1967.

4.4 Hutchings, P. "Can We Say that Omniscience is Impossible?" *Australasian Journal of Philosophy*, XLI (1962–63), pp. 394–396. [Discussion of 4.13].

4.5 Kretzmann, Norman. "Omniscience and Immutability," *The Journal of Philosophy*, LXIII (1966), pp. 409–421.

4.6 Lachs, J. "Professor Prior on Omniscience," *Philosophy*, XXXVIII (1963), pp. 361–364. [Discussion of 4.9].

4.7 Pike, Nelson. "Divine Omniscience and Voluntary Action," *Philosophical Review*, LXXIV (1965), pp. 27–46.

4.8 — — —. "Of God and Freedom: A Rejoinder," *Philosophical Review*, LXXV (1966), pp. 369–379. [Discussion of 4.14].

4.9 Prior, Arthur N. "The Formalities of Omniscience," *Philosophy*, XXXVIII (1963), pp. 114–129.

4.10 — — —. "Reply to Mr. Lachs," *Philosophy*, XXXVIII (1963), pp. 365-366. [Discussion of 4.6].

4.11 — — —. *Past, Present, and Future*. Oxford: Clarendon Press, 1967.

4.12 — — —. *Papers on Time and Tense*. New York: Oxford University Press, 1968.

4.13 Puccetti, R. "Is Omniscience Possible?" *Australasian Journal of Philosophy*, XLI (1962–63), pp. 92–93.

4.14 Saunders, John Turk. "Of God and Freedom," *Philosophical Review*, LXXV (1966), pp. 219–225. [Discussion of 4.7].

*4.15 Taylor, Richard. "Determinism," *The Encyclopedia of Philosophy*, ed. Edwards, P., Vol. II, pp. 359–373. New York: The Macmillan Co. and The Free Press, 1967.

4.16 — — —. "Fatalism," *Philosophical Review*, LXXI (1962), pp. 56–66.

4.17 — — —. "A Note on Fatalism," *Philosophical Review*, LXXII (1963), pp. 497–499.

4.18 — — —. *Metaphysics*, Chapter 5, "Fate," pp. 54–69. Englewood Cliffs, N.J.: Prentice-Hall, 1963.

5. RECENT DISCUSSIONS OF ARISTOTLE'S *DE INTERPRETATIONE*, CHAPTER 9

*5.1 Ackrill, J. L. Notes in his *Aristotle's Categories and De Interpretatione: Translated with Notes*. ("Clarendon Aristotle Series"). Oxford: Clarendon Press, 1963.

*5.2 Albritton, Rogers. "Present Truth and Future Contingency," *Philosophical Review*, LXVI (1957), pp. 29–46.

5.3 Amand, David. *Fatalisme et liberté dans l'antiquité grecque*. Louvain: Bibliothèque de l'Université, 1945.

*5.4 Anscombe, G. E. M. "Aristotle and the Sea-Battle," *Mind*, LXV (1956), pp. 1–15.

5.5 Ayer, A. J. "Fatalism," in his *The Concept of a Person and Other Essays*. London: Macmillan, 1963.

5.6 Baylis, Charles A. "Are Some Propositions neither True nor False?" *Philosophy of Science*, III (1936), pp. 156–166.

5.7 Becker, O. "Bestreitet Aristoteles die Gültigkeit des 'Tertium non datur' für Zukunftsaussagen?" *Actes du Congrès International de Philosophie Scientifique*, VI (1936), pp. 69–74.

5.8 — — —. *Die aristotelische Theorie der Möglichkeitsschlüsse*. Berlin: Junker und Dünnhaupt, 1933.

5.9 Bradley, R. D. "Must the Future Be What It Is Going To Be?" *Mind*, LXVIII (1959), pp. 193–208.

5.10 Butler, Ronald J. "Aristotle's Sea Fight and Three-Valued Logic," *Philosophical Review*, LXIV (1955), pp. 264–274.

5.11 Cahn, Steven M. *Fate, Logic, and Time*. New Haven: Yale University Press, 1967.

5.12 Grant, C. K. "Certainty, Necessity, and Aristotle's Sea Battle," *Mind*, LXVI (1957), pp. 522–531. [Discussion of 5.4].

5.13 Hartshorne, Charles. "The Meaning of 'Is Going to Be'," *Mind*, LXXIV (1965), pp. 46–58. [Discussion of 5.9, 5.22].

5.14 Hintikka, Jaakko. "Aristotle and the 'Master Argument' of Diodorus," *American Philosophical Quarterly*, I (1964), pp. 101–114.

5.15 – – –. "Necessity, Universality, and Time in Aristotle," *Ajatus*, XX (1957), pp. 65–90.

5.16 – – –. "The Once and Future Sea Fight," *Philosophical Review*, LXXIII (1964), pp. 461–492.

5.17 Ihrig, A. H. "Remarks on Logical Necessity and Future Contingencies," *Mind*, LXXIV (1965), pp. 215–228.

5.18 King-Farlow, John. "Sea-Fights without Tears," *Analysis*, XIX (1958–59), pp. 36–42.

5.19 Kneale, William and Kneale, Martha. Part II, Section 4 (pp. 45–54) in their *The Development of Logic*. Oxford: Clarendon Press, 1962.

5.20 Linsky, Leonard. "Professor Donald Williams on Aristotle," *Philosophical Review*, LXIII (1954), pp. 250–252. [Discussion of 5.36].

5.21 Lukasiewicz, Jan. *Aristotle's Syllogistic from the Standpoint of Modern Formal Logic*. Second Edition. Oxford: Clarendon Press, 1957.

5.22 Montague, R. "Mr. Bradley on the Future," *Mind*, LXIX (1960), pp. 550–554. [Discussion of 5.9].

5.23 Patzig, Günther. *Die aristotelische Syllogistik. (Abhandlungen der Akademie der Wissenschaften in Göttingen, Philologisch-historische Klasse, Dritte Folge*, Nr. 42). Göttingen: Vandenhoeck und Ruprecht, 1959.

5.24 Pears, David. "Time, Truth, and Inference," *Proceedings of the Aristotelian Society*, LI (1950–51), pp. 1–24. (Reprinted in Antony Flew (ed.), *Essays in Conceptual Analysis*. London: Macmillan, 1956).

5.25 Prior, Arthur N. "Three-Valued Logic and Future Contingents," *Philosophical Quarterly*, III (1953), pp. 317–326.

5.26 – – –. *Time and Modality*. Oxford: Clarendon Press, 1957.

5.27 – – –. "The Sea-Battle Tomorrow," Part III, Chapter II, Section 2 (pp. 240–250) in his *Formal Logic*. Oxford: Clarendon Press, 1955. [Discussion of Ockham as well as of Aristotle].

5.28 Rescher, Nicholas. "An Interpretation of Aristotle's Doctrine of Future Contingency and Excluded Middle," in his *Studies in the History of Arabic Logic.* Pittsburgh, University of Pittsburgh Press, 1963.

5.29 Ryle, Gilbert. Chapter II in his *Dilemmas.* Cambridge: Cambridge University Press, 1954.

5.30 Saunders, John Turk. "A Sea Fight Tomorrow?" *Philosophical Review*, LXVII (1958), pp. 367–379.

5.31 Schuhl, Pierre-Maxime. *Le dominateur et les possibles.* (Especially appendices I and IV). Paris: Presses Universitaires de France, 1960.

5.32 Strang, Colin. "Aristotle and the Sea Battle," *Mind*, LXIX (1960), pp. 447–465.

*5.33 Taylor, Richard. "The Problem of Future Contingencies," *Philosophical Review*, LXVI (1957), pp. 1–28.

5.34 — — —. [Same as 4.16 above].

5.35 — — —. [Same as 4.17 above].

5.36 Williams, Donald C. "The Sea Fight Tomorrow," in Paul Henle *et al.* (eds.), *Structure, Method and Meaning.* New York: Liberal Arts Press, 1951.

5.37 — — —. "Professor Linsky on Aristotle," *Philosophical Review*, LXIII (1954), pp. 253–255. [Discussion of 5.20].

5.38 Wolff, P. "Truth, Futurity, and Contingency," *Mind*, LXIX (1960), pp. 398–402. [Discussion of 5.9].

SUPPLEMENTAL BIBLIOGRAPHY

Celluprica, Vincenza. *Il Capitolo 9 del "De interpretatione" di Aristotele: Rassegna di studi 1930–1973.* Urbino: Società editrice il Mulino, 1977.

Knuuttila, Simo, ed. *Reforging the Great Chain of Being: Studies of the History of Modal Theories.* Dordrecht: Reidel, 1981.

— — —. "Modal Logic," Ch. 17 in *The Cambridge History of Later Medieval Philosophy*, ed. N. Kretzmann, A. Kenny, and J. Pinborg; Cambridge: Cambridge University Press, 1982.

Normore, Calvin. "Future Contingents," Ch. 18 in *The Cambridge History of Later Medieval Philosophy*.

INDEX